TIDELINE

Captains, Fly-Fishing, and the American Coast

TIDELINE

Captains, Fly-Fishing, and the American Coast

Kirk D. Deeter and Andrew W. Steketee

Photographs by Marco Lorenzetti

Willow Creek Press

Dedication

This book is dedicated to our sons: Paul Gustavo, Charlie, Carlo, Marco Paul, and Lorenzo.

Acknowledgments

We gratefully acknowledge the support of our families, friends and colleagues.
We particularly want to thank Sarah Deeter for her efforts and understanding —
And our editorial assistant, Stephanie Aromando, for attending to the details.

Published by Willow Creek Press
P.O. Box 147, Minocqua, Wisconsin 54548

Editor: Andrea K. Donner

Library of Congress Cataloging-in-Publication Data
Deeter, Kirk D.
Tideline : captains, fly-fishing, and the American coastline / by Kirk Deeter and Andrew Steketee ;
photography by Marco Lorenzetti.
p. cm.
ISBN 1-57223-701-5 (hardcover : alk. paper)
1. Fishing guides--United States. 2. Saltwater fly fishing--United States--Anecdotes. I. Steketee, Andrew W., 1967- II. Title.
SH456.2.D44 2004
799.16--dc22
2004002255

Printed in Canada

Contents

Prologue

It seemed like the right thing to do at the time.

It was a Sunday afternoon in October 2002. I was standing somewhere on the North Fork of the South Platte River. My waders were leaking. It was snowing, or more appropriately "icing," and I was wishing for a hatch that wasn't going to happen. Standing there with frost-caked eyelids, red windburned cheeks, a dripping nose, and frozen fingers, I dunked my fly rod in the

current, trying in vain to clear ice clumps from its guides, then simply bowed my head in self disgust.

"Man, there's something terribly wrong with this picture," I thought. "I've had enough of this. I deserve a change of scenery, with sun and beaches, and warm, calm oceans, and big fish. Yeah, that's right, fish like marlin, and sharks, and tarpon, and redfish. And when I'm done catching these fish, I'll lounge with my toes in the sand, eat shrimp, drink rum punch… the kind with real fruit and a paper umbrella… and watch the brilliant sunsets. Yeah…"

"Hey dude, you mind if I fish here?" Another yahoo jumped in the river directly in front of me, then waded out and stood in the middle of the run. At least he asked.

"And solitude. God, I need solitude." The daydream had become a prayer.

And then it hit me, as if the skies parted and a single beam of sunlight shone down on my little ski cap to warm up the next big idea. I already had produced one fishing book, *Castwork: Reflections of Fly-Fishing Guides and the American West*, with Andrew and Liz Steketee (who are brother and sister). It was, admittedly, a five-year hobby and an excuse to go fishing. But it turned out pretty well, and we earned some positive credit for having delved into an interesting slice of Americana, ultimately revealing glimpses at the working characters and culture of western fly-fishing in a way that hadn't been done before.

I'd take that template to saltwater. No problem. All I had to do was sell the idea to my editor and publisher, then convince two partners to spend a summer on the road, find a collection of great saltwater guides with interesting stories (who would donate time to the project), conceive of a way to make this book different from yet equally compelling as the first, iron out some logistics, and it was a done deal…

Fast forward one year. It is amazing that everything worked out. But things did not happen the way anyone had expected when the project was planned.

There were some significant technical differences between the first book and this one, though the underlying premise was basically the same. That premise was to study the "working soul" of sport fishing by following people who make a living on the water. Ultimately, we expected to see how people

and landscapes, or seascapes, are reflections of each other. We certainly did not intend to write a how-to book or a travel journal. We simply wanted to capture, in prose and photography, a sense of "what is" putting you, the reader, in the boats, letting you taste the experiences, and perhaps prompting you to draw your own conclusions.

How we went about this book was totally new. First, and most obviously, this photography belongs to Marco Lorenzetti, who brought his own vision and technical approach to the project. He shot all the images in medium or large format, and in doing so, created a more detailed compendium of work in which every picture tells its own story. In that same sense, we wrote this text as a mosaic of sorts, in that each section paints its own picture of a certain time, place, or character in the overall experience.

Because saltwater was a relatively new realm for us (I was the only one who had fly-fished saltwater before this book, and that experience was limited to a dozen or so days of snook and tarpon fishing, one bonefishing trip to Belize, and another sailfishing trip I had done on assignment for *Wild on the Fly* in Guatemala), we collectively went into this project with wide eyes and few, if any, preconceived notions. We finished the project with a healthy respect for this game, and a realization of how much there is to learn and understand in saltwater. In that regard, we felt it more appropriate to end each chapter with a short vignette, written by Andrew, on the experience, rather than notes or tips on fishing techniques, considering we were learning on the job.

It is worth noting that we made all nine trips within six months, beginning with Bill Curtis in Miami on March 8, and finishing with Conway Bowman in San Diego on August 29, 2003. Andrew and I would fly from Colorado, Marco typically would drive from Detroit, and we would meet to spend three or four days at each location. Admittedly, we could have included other places and other subjects, but we felt the locations we chose balanced the overall project, and, perhaps more importantly, made our production timeline feasible.

Because the project was basically a "summer tour," it seemed fitting to infuse a little more of our personal adventure into the overall narrative, though you will notice that we maintained the use of an anonymous, plural first person voice in order to keep the focus on the guides (captains) as much as possible.

The overall process of producing this book proved to be an eye-opening, sometimes painful, ultimately rewarding experience. There were behind-the-scenes moments that I still replay in my mind like clips from highlight reels: Marco and Andrew staring with mouths hanging wide open the first time we jumped a tarpon with Bill Curtis; being stranded on the Florida turnpike when the transmission on Bill's Astro broke; a Louisiana backyard fish grill with Gary Taylor; Mexican food—the real deal—with Chuck Naiser and Tim Clancey (the boss at New Water Boat Works, who ran our chase skiff); eight days in New England and New York during which I was dry maybe 30 minutes total; early mornings and unmentionable jokes with Rick Murphy; bugs and wicked storms with Al Keller; and kicking back at Dana Landing with Conway Bowman and his father.

Mixing those experiences with cut fingers, jammed cameras, broken rods (four), cheap beer, bouncy flights, empty highways, seasickness, bug bites, sunburn, thirst, three cases of the homesick blues, and many other things that never will be printed, I now realize that we "bled" on this project. And that is my fault. But it seemed like the right thing to do at the time.

We never came anywhere close to the toes-in-the-sand and rum punches with little umbrellas. And now, I am not captivated by the allure of saltwater fishing as much as I am held hostage by it. I love its grittiness, its character, and I am eager to face the world of challenges it presents. Most of all, I love the saltwater fishing culture. My hope is that we are able to convey some level of this essence in the pages that follow.

I undoubtedly will be back on the flats or out in bluewater, but probably not until after I'm done licking my wounds. I think I'll fish the Platte tomorrow.

Kirk D. Deeter
Pine, Colorado
November 2003

Bill Curtis

Miami, Florida

Early on a hot March morning, we find ourselves standing outside the Miami Dadeland Marriott hotel, waiting for the odyssey to begin.

Our friends had told us we should start this book project with Bill Curtis. They said most of what we would see in the coming months had been, at least in part, created, improvised, explained, or experienced by Curtis. He is, by unanimous account, one of the fathers of saltwater flats fishing, and one of the last living legends of this game. But the best part of the story is that Bill Curtis, now in his late seventies, is still playing it.

He arrives, five minutes early, in a Chevy Astro Minivan, pulling a canary yellow skiff, the "Grasshopper," straight through the mix of valets and bellhops, who trade confused glances as he wheels up to the front door, occupying both lanes of traffic, and stops. He rolls down his passenger side window, barks at the doorman, then asks us if we're here to fish. Before we have time to answer, he opens the van's back doors and is loading equipment. Eventually, we would learn that Bill Curtis does things his way, and the rest of the world can deal with that.

We pack up and head out into traffic toward the Dixie Highway. A half-century ago, when Bill moved here, this neighborhood was on the far, rural edge of Miami, but today, it is consumed with the sprawl of strip malls, shopping centers, office complexes, and car dealerships. If not for the palm trees on the roadside, you might think you were in suburban Detroit or Denver. We are a moving anachronism, pulling Bill's little yellow boat through six lanes of traffic.

Nobody says much beyond introductions, until he asks where we want to start. We don't have one answer.

We want him to open his bag of tricks

and teach us to fish, anywhere. More importantly, we want him to tell us how the whole story started—poling the Everglades with a long, wooden dowel and a weathered plywood skiff, the enormous schools of tarpon and bonefish that since have disappeared, a day fishing with Ted Williams, what it was like to be the only boat on Biscayne Bay—but where does it really begin?

"I'll tell you what," says Bill. "We'll head down to Flamingo, drop the boat in the water, and see if we can't see some tarpon rollin'. Your story will begin on the water. They always do."

We launch from the outside ramp and run past Palm and Cormorant Keys into the northern reaches of Florida Bay, then Bill sets up in a channel near a mangrove island swarming with roseate spoonbills. He wants to see if we can fish before he starts talking. It seems we are on the spit to start out, as he begins to interview us with rods, not words. As he eloquently explains, "There's chicken salad and chicken shit, and you can't make chicken salad out of chicken shit."

We find a mixed bag of small jacks, spotted seatrout, ladyfish, and pompano, throwing gaudy, rattling "Cajun Thunders" and shrimp-tipped jigs into the channel with spinning rods. In doing so, we extract some of Bill's basic history. He tells us he is from eastern Oklahoma, and learned to fish in New Mexico in 1934, throwing Adams flies with split-cane rods on the San Juan River under the guidance of his uncle. He even held the world record for rainbow trout on six-pound tippet for a fish he caught up in Alaska, but could care less, when we ask, about its length and weight.

He served in the Army Air Corps during World War II, piloting F-7's on photoreconnaissance missions over North Africa. Bill says it was when he returned to base with holes in his wings and fuselage large enough for the maintenance crews to climb through that "he knew he was immortal." After the war, he became a professional photographer in south Florida, shooting assignments for the J. Walter Thompson Agency, but eventually, his passion for fishing led him to the relatively uncharted realm of the flats. He began guiding in 1958.

There are other guides, contemporaries, who have received more attention and

acclaim than Bill over the years. There was a feature in *Sports Illustrated* back in the 1960s, and a permit show for the original "American Sportsman," not long after that, but Bill did not enter the profession to become a star. He says he was drawn by the work, the fish, and the experience, and never spent a whole lot of time worrying about getting noticed.

"Maybe the biggest compliment and the most credit I got was when the young guides used to set on the flats and watch me with binoculars," laughs Bill. "Hell, there's now more than 100 registered guides in Islamorada alone. Being a fishing guide is no big deal, but I take some pride in being one of the people who was here when this thing took off."

"Well, I'd better get on the stick," says Bill, gingerly climbing onto the poling platform. *Whoosh, whoosh.* The sound of the push pole sliding through Bill's calloused and worn hands makes a distinct sound, like a dry eraser rubbing up and down a chalkboard. His deftness on the platform almost defies logic, but when we learn he is the inventor of said contraption, his surprising agility begins to make more sense.

"I used to stand on the motor to spot fish, but it wasn't very steady, so I decided to make a little stand bolted to risers off the deck," he explains. "I remember at first how some of the other guides laughed at me, and thought I had put a fish cleaning table on the boat. I just told them it was to shade my motor."

Whether they realize it or not, many of today's guides have been influenced by Bill Curtis. He has designed and developed shallow water boats like the Hewes Bonefisher, the first production flats boat; tested products for the Ted Williams Tackle Company; introduced and created indispensable fishing knots, including the "Bimini Twist" (which he brought to Florida) and the "Curtis Connection" (his own invention); and made countless other improvements to tackle and technique during his 50 years in the sport. If you look hard enough, you will notice his contributions marking the flats boats of the world like indelible fingerprints.

Watching Bill's hands tie intricate knots is like watching an old maestro play the piano with fingers slowed by age (but nonetheless, graceful and deliberate as they pass over the keys). Bill says the best anglers have natural grace, and he never has fished with anyone more graceful than the late Ted Williams, the finest hitter in the history of baseball.

"Hell, Williams claimed he could see the stitches on a baseball coming at him, and I believed him," remembers Bill. "He had perfect coordination, superior vision, and he could transpose his athletic grace to anything, including fishing. He won the first two Gold Cup Tournaments, and then stopped fishing them, just so others could have a chance. He was the first man to make athlete and fisherman fit in the same sentence."

The next day, we are ripping across Biscayne Bay toward the tarpon, bonefish, and permit flats on the east side. With his white, sunworn knuckles loosely rolled over the wheel and the throttle wide open, Bill Curtis is in his element. He has guided everywhere from the Bahamas to the Dry Tortugas, from Flamingo to the Keys, from the Crystal River to north of Homassasa, but this is his home water, and where he made his name.

"I was the only one guiding here back in the early days," says Curtis. "There were a few others working down in the Keys, like Jimmy Albright and Al Smith, but this is what I was known for, bonefish and tarpon in Biscayne Bay."

He also played a significant role in the preservation of these fish and these remarkably productive flats. Bill helped found Bonefish and Tarpon Unlimited, and recounts for our benefit former trips in the early 1960s, scouting and fishing with Stewart Udall, then Secretary of the Interior, and Luther Hodges, the Secretary of Commerce.

"Jack Kennedy was President," Bill shouts over the whining engine. "And we were laying the groundwork for designating Biscayne Bay a National Park. Of course, back then, this was still a pretty wild place, and you always could find a piece of water without having to fight over it."

We watch a cigarette boat tear across the horizon. It is one of hundreds of watercraft—party boats, ski boats, WaveRunners, sailboats, even dozens of undaunted anglers—crisscrossing and running through the fragile, mottled green waters of the bay. Bill had told us to expect this as we waited in line to launch his skiff at the public landing. It is still worth seeing, he said, and who knows, we might run into a bonefish or permit if we head far enough south. Anyway, he has a special place he wants to show us.

"This is it," he says, as he slows the engine, rounding the southern tip of a mangrove island and pointing toward the open Atlantic. "This is Curtis Point."

"Back in the 50s and 60s, there were 20 times more fish than we have here today," he reflects. "I can remember seeing a school of tarpon that stretched an eighth of a mile wide, maybe a quarter mile long, as they funneled along this point. We hooked an 80-pounder at the head, fought the fish nearly 30 minutes, and watched the whole time as the rest of the school flooded by the boat. Hell, all you had to do was get your line in the water, and it would've been impossible for a tarpon not to have eaten your fly."

As Bill reflects on the experience, he adds, "We won't ever see schools of fish like that again."

Retreating from Curtis Point, we find a hidden bay where the dense, waving turtlegrass yields to white sand depressions, aligned across the bottom like triangular white fingers on a backgammon board. It doesn't look like anyone has been here, at least not for a few hours.

"We'll stake off and see if we can't make something happen," Bill says. "These bonefish run off the flats on a low slack tide, but move back in on the incoming. The water's coming up, so we might try it."

He reaches into the storage chest and pulls out a small hand-crank food processor, tosses in a fistful of brown shrimp, and starts grinding. When finished, he takes two heaping handfuls of ground up protein and throws them off the front of the boat. Bill explains that when loud boat motors send the nervous bonefish running for deeper water, it sometimes takes a little "special sauce" to coax them into playing.

The fish finding game may have changed over the past 40 years, but most of the fundamentals, like the bonefish cast, have not. Bill tells us to keep a low profile, and leave our casting hands below our shoulders. He picks up the rod and starts wiggling it overhead to illustrate his point. The dropping afternoon sun exaggerates the rod's shadow. He says any change in light, caused by a bird gliding overhead, a passing cloud, and particularly a flagging fly rod, will signal danger to the bonefish, and scare them off.

"When you raise your rod hand overhead, it's like you're waving hello to the fish before you cast at him, and he likely won't wave back," explains Bill. "When everything lines up just right, it'll feel like you've

hooked the bottom, but that bottom will start moving away at 45 miles-an-hour."

We wait, drink some water, and wait some more.

A lone permit slinks out of the dark grass and onto the scoured out basin where Bill had thrown the last handful of minced shrimp. Bill, eating a sandwich with nonchalance, is the first to notice the fish. We are none the wiser until he shuffles up toward the front of the boat to get a closer look, then starts mumbling to himself through a full cheek of ham and cheese, "twenty Goddamned pounds of something-or-other, standing out like the ace of spades."

"It's a permit alright. You might as well give him a shot, because he won't stick around for long," Bill says, tossing the last chunk of sandwich overboard.

We wind up with two false casts, off to the side, then drop the fly at the target. It looks like a pretty decent shot—in front of the fish, maybe a foot long, but not bad. The permit tilts down slowly to inspect the fly and refuses. Annoyed, confused, or amused the 25-pound permit turns, momentarily, to reveal his pale chrome flank, like a beat up trash can lid, then vanishes into the grass.

Bill isn't surprised, and he isn't disappointed. Of all the fish on the flats, permit are the most fickle and unpredictable. You usually only get one shot, and they are notorious for refusing the fly, even when the cast is perfect. Bill has witnessed this routine many, many times, enough not to expect their cooperation, or believe in beginner's luck.

"These permit know the difference between meat and potatoes," Bill utters.

"Was the cast okay?" we ask, seeking to rationalize failure, or find some level of approval from our captain.

"Fair," answers Bill. "You might want to soften the delivery up. Most fish aren't used to their food attacking them. You haven't ever eaten anything that was looking to bite you in the ass have you?"

Almost all good writing on Florida flats fishing—especially stories on the uniquely gritty, sometimes cutthroat guiding culture of the Keys—reflects, intentionally or not, the persona of Bill Curtis. It is hard to read any story about this area's fly-fishing heydays, turf wars, wild adventures, or working character, without somehow seeing Bill Curtis in the pages.

Bill likes writers, or so he says. He tells us about days on the water with Karl Hiassen, and recounts a prolonged tarpon battle with Jim Harrison, a fight that only ended as night fell, when both men conceded the fish would drag them to Mexico if they didn't cut it off. Bill's favorite story involves another writer and angler with whom he had a run-in near Key West, roughly thirty years ago.

"He had a 17-foot center console Mako, and decided to race me for this little channel, but my Hewes Bonefisher was just a little faster. So I made the cut before he did, trimming up my engine so he would eat my spray as I ran across Northwest Channel. When we got into Garrison Bight, I really hosed him out.

"I didn't know who he was at the time, but he knew me, so he came around looking to start something back at the dock. I had a charter with me, a guy and his wife, but he ran right over, all mad, and started yelling, 'if you do that again you son-of-a-bitch, I'll…

"And I said, 'fine, you just come down right now, and we'll start swingin',' but one way or another, it blew over."

Some time later, mutual friends would introduce Bill Curtis to Thomas McGuane. They eventually forged their own, respectful friendship.

"He got to be a pretty famous writer and a decent friend," says Bill. "He invited me to a party at his house once, where I met Jimmy Buffett, and he even offered to get me up to Montana to fish the Boulder and Yellowstone Rivers, but I haven't taken him up on that yet."

Early on the last day, Bill stashes the push pole, and kicks on the electric trolling motor to slide us along the east edge of Oyster Bay. Although the water is discolored, there are droves of 100-pound tarpon rolling and crashing ladyfish across the flat. As we blind cast, Bill says to be patient and keep working ahead of the boat, it will pay off sooner or later.

"Nice cast," Bill shouts down from the platform. "Now shoot another on the backhand, ahead of these fish rolling at three o'clock." When Bill Curtis says "nice cast," it is tall praise, and certainly enough to keep the faith and the effort going. "Come on 'poons…eat the fly," he utters.

Suddenly, there is rock-hard tension at the end of the line. The tarpon grabs the Greenie Weenie, only 20 feet from the boat, and gives us a jaw-dropping first glance, flashing below the stained surface like a sunken, aluminum canoe. Time stands still, long enough for everyone, except Bill, to trade wide-eyed, startled glances as the fish rolls in the tannic water and starts pulling away from the boat. We set the hook just like Bill told us—three short, hard tugs to the side, like a hammer driving nails into fresh wood.

The tarpon makes three successive, greyhounding jumps, and each time we bow to the fish, so he won't spit the hook or break us off. But shock turns to panic when we realize there is a problem: The wind has blown a few loose coils of fly line across the deck, and tangled them around the stashed push pole. Three hands scramble to twist loose the spaghetti-like mess, but the fish already is streaking into Oyster Bay. In another second, the tarpon is off, busting the 50-pound leader like an afterthought.

"It happens," says Bill, quietly. He offers

consolation, but cannot hide his own disappointment. Then he gathers the fly line and starts the long process of building a new leader. He tosses us another fly from the box and tells us to start sharpening it.

Megalops atlanticus, the tarpon, is among the most sought-after gamefish on the Florida flats for its strength, size, and remarkably acrobatic fighting style. One hook up, one jump will have visions of the "silver king" cartwheeling through your dreams for the rest of your angling life. With large, armor-plated scales and gills, a deeply forked tail, and a mouth like an upturned trap door, tarpon are prehistoric creatures.

Nearly unevolved from 100,000 years ago, they still swim with mystery and wonder. Only recently have scientists discovered that they are among the longest-living fish in the ocean. By measuring the carbon deposits on the otoliths (earbones) of tarpon, a process akin to carbon dating dinosaur fossils, experts now know that tarpon can live for 50 years or longer. It seems strange to imagine the possibility that Bill Curtis could catch a tarpon today that was born before he began guiding in 1958.

In addition to breathing through gills, tarpon also have evolved the amazing ability to breathe in poorly oxygenated waters by breaking the surface and gulping air; the ingested oxygen is passed along to a highly specialized swim bladder where it is dispersed throughout the fish's blood stream. Scientists are unclear whether this unique breathing ability is an adaptation for juvenile survival (allowing the young to avoid predators in low saline back waters), or a means for adults to exploit the rich, brackish feeding grounds of many estuarine environments.

Even the where, when, and how of tarpon spawning are uncertain, though scientists do know that they engage in a primal, pre-spawn ritual where groups of fish swim in symmetrical, head-to-tail circles called "daisy chains." Bill recounts how he once found himself in the middle of three, nonintersecting (externally tangent) daisy chains near Homosassa in the late 60s, and simply sat and watched the hypnotic motions of hundreds and hundreds of fish without making a cast. In all his years, he only has seen this occur once.

It is clear that Bill has enormous respect for the tarpon.

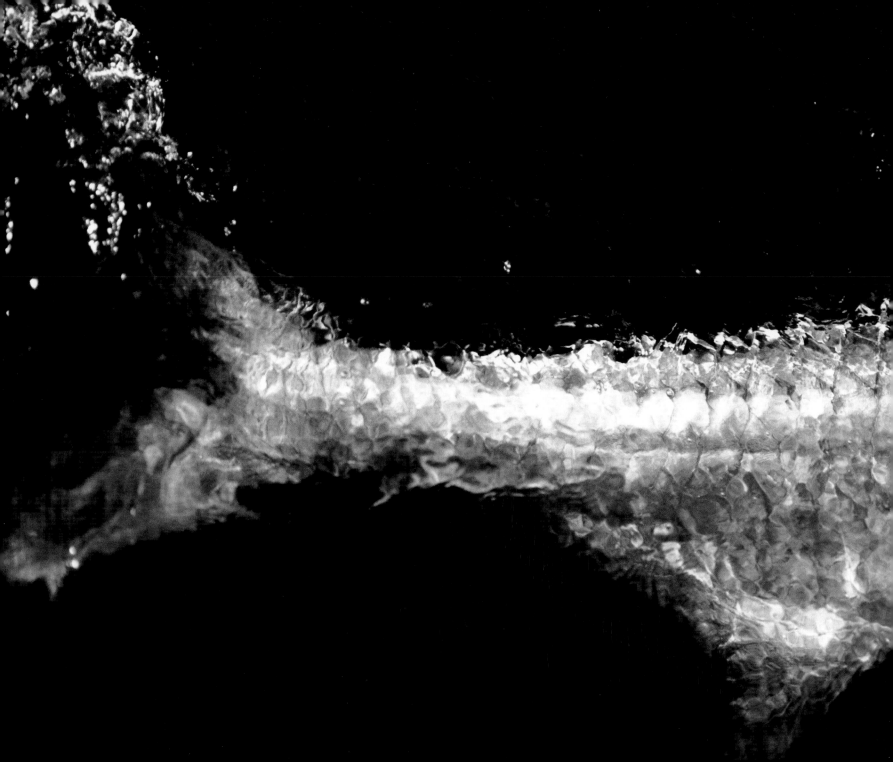

"To me, tarpon are the top of the game, the ultimate gamefish," says Bill. "I read stories about people going after sailfish and tuna on the fly and so on, but when first-timers catch a party boat fish like that, they still don't know what the hell they're doing. You have to be pretty damn good and skilled to hook a tarpon, and landing one is even tougher. I know more than one good angler who has had a bad laundry moment after tangling with the silver king."

Driving home from the Everglades on our final afternoon, we feel more than satisfied having fished and learned from Bill Curtis for three days. We feel honored. It is as if we had just played three rounds of golf at Augusta with Arnold Palmer. Bill Curtis has been more than gracious, more than patient, and, in return, our respect for his game has grown tenfold. It is matched only by our respect for the man, and the beautiful, fragile waters where he has worked for all these years.

Back at Bill's modest house, watching him tie original tarpon patterns, we notice that the man and these places he has poured his blood and sweat into have become reflections of each other. Like wind and rain carving away at sandstone, time and overuse slowly have worn down Bill, the Everglades, Biscayne Bay, and the Keys.

In reality, some estimate that 90 percent of the reefs in the Keys have died in the time that Bill Curtis has lived here. The Everglades are depleted, burdened by water diversions, development, agriculture, drought, fires, and more.

"I only hope the Everglades come halfway back to what they were 50 years ago, before I die," says Bill.

At least there is hope, and more than that, resilience. Resilience in the land and in the man, to keep fighting on, keep pressing forward, and keep running one step ahead of time. There also is a lesson, and now a legacy, which cannot be conveyed in passages from a book, in a movie, or on television. The lesson and the legacy are about grace and perseverance, about growing old with honor, and about battling the elements, the fish, for as long as you can.

At nearly eighty years of age, Captain Bill Curtis still is chasing 120-pound tarpon on Oyster Bay. When the time comes, how many of us will be able to make that claim?

Permit Failing

In Biscayne Bay it is smart to let the permit find you,
otherwise, you're hunting witches or stars in the afternoon.
Captain swears brown rancid snapping shrimp milled
from a dirty livewell then pitched into the rising tide
will get a hungry, fender colored permit up on the flats,
but that's no guarantee he'll eat or even look at your fly.
Ninety-nine out of a hundred permit know the difference
between meat and potatoes, and the one that doesn't,
he's either stupid or you're lucky to catch him at all.
Anyhow, feeding permit is like feeding pigeons,
just chum and wait, hardly work involved, no real talent,
like you went to church to pray then started begging.
Hang on, there's a real decent permit, twenty-five pounds,
maybe better, coming to look at your fly. You might pray now.

Chuck Naiser

Rockport, Texas

Driving south from Houston on a flat two-lane, heat mirages ripple the highway concrete, a Coke can sweats in the dashboard cup holder, and a light wind folds the tops of hundred-year-old trees. We can't see Aransas Bay yet, but we know we are close. We can smell saltwater in the breeze.

Thick oaks and scrubs are bent like blades of fresh cut grass in a gnarled symmetry, unanimously stretched at even angles to the northwest. The trees are living monuments to the power of the Gulf Coast's wind and water, clear roadside reminders that the ocean ultimately has its way with the land, even in Texas.

On the car stereo, we rifle through songs by our favorite Lone Star troubadours: Robert Earl Keen, Jerry Jeff Walker, Terry Allen, Jimmie Dale Gilmore, Lyle Lovett, and, of course, Willie Nelson. Finally, we land on a tune by Guy Clark that seems to resonate the subtleties of this expansive landscape we have wandered into.

"The south coast of Texas is a thin slice of life – It's salty and hard, it is stern as a knife – Where the wind is for blowin' up hurricanes for showin' – The snakes how to swim and the trees how to lean."

"And the shrimpers and their ladies are out in the beer joints – Drinkin' 'em down for they sail with the dawn – They're bound for the Mexican Bay of Campeche – and the deck hands are singin' adios Jolé Blon."

Rolling the final few miles past Tex-Mex burrito stands, weathered seafood shacks, and liquor stores, we concede that there won't be any whooping it up tonight, save a few pounds of boiled shrimp and a Shiner or two, before knocking off to the clatter of an air conditioner in a roadside motel room. In the morning, we will be stalking redfish in the tidal lakes and channels near Rockport with Chuck Naiser.

He had warned us to be rested. We will be walking many hard miles through muck, snake grass, and briny water; fighting wind, tides, and sun; and making hundreds of long, difficult casts to elusive, tailing redfish.

"This ain't Florida or Louisiana," Chuck warned us. "This is Texas, and we'll be stalking these fish for our shots. You know what they say about everything in Texas being bigger…well, you boys have never seen flats like these before."

We meet Chuck the next morning at his bayside house, and our dress-down starts before sunup. First, he rips into us about our wimpy (ankle-less) wading boots, which he calls "slippers," then asks if we have packed our pink tutus. Next, he begins bouncing around the dock with arms flapping like some crazed Amazon ballerina in song, laughing and lisping, "I'm afraid of redfish, I'm afraid of redfish."

When we finally load the boat, Chuck fires up the engine and planes off into the stiff morning breeze. He turns and shouts over the engine at one of us: "Darlin' get your hand off your hat. You look like a damned tourist."

We like Chuck from the get-go. He has a twinkle in his eye, bear-mitt hands, and a genuine Texas demeanor, the kind where that 'ol boy can slap his hand on your back (hard), look straight into your eyes, and call you a "som-bytch" with a grin. Your only response is to look right back at him and smile.

Chuck Naiser is all about fun, though it is clear from the outset he is not to be underestimated. He likely is smarter than you are, unquestionably stronger, and no doubt tougher. He carries out his daily routine, mixing equal parts of sarcasm and purpose, smiling, never pressuring, and always pressing forward. For him, guiding isn't a job or a hobby. It is a way of life.

The key to this way of life, says Chuck, is to keep things simple, to focus on things the angler can control, and accept the things we cannot. Life, for Chuck, is meant to be experienced, not influenced. He says, we aren't put here on this earth to worry about every little detail.

"Boys, there are two things in life I

don't do. I don't tie flies, and I don't distill scotch. I like 'em both good enough, but I haven't the time to make either."

We glide around a cordgrass point, sidestep a duck blind, and Chuck kills the engine. The back channel water is milky, and streaked with orange glints from a slow-walking sun. He is sure there are fish back here, even if we cannot see them yet. He stamps his foot on the skiff's white deck, and the channel erupts in electric boils. A hidden school of fish reacts like it has been goosed by a cattle prod.

"Oh, we in 'em now, darlin'," he whispers.

Chuck says these fish are just "pups," and the bigger ones will be out in the middle of the pond, where we will have to sneak up on them. Time to start walking. Chuck grabs his fishing kit and slips over the side of the boat into the lukewarm water. He already has plotted a course to cut off the bigger school: Up over a hump of grass, around the bay's windward edge, and back into the vein of current where the reds likely are feeding.

He is moving quickly, but quietly, eyes trained forward. There is no more teasing. Instruction is pointed, clear, and succinct. We must hustle to avoid being lost in his wake.

"Walk right behind me."

"Huh?"

"Snakes."

"Oh."

"Shuffle your feet in this muddy water."

"What?"

"Stingrays."

"Yes sir."

We crest the grass mound and walk onto the flat. Chuck wants roughly 50 feet of line stripped out, and everyone ready for his call. When he says "go," he expects one backcast and a fly in the water, preferably near a feeding redfish.

Chuck sees the redfish. We cannot. For us, the water is a confusing myriad of wind-blown rivulets and currents, broken sticks and waving, matted grass. Everything that moves—wind, waves, bait, blue crabs, even cloud shadows—looks like the movements of redfish. Mullet splash to the left, and we swing our heads in that direction. A gull dives to the right, and we swivel that way. Chuck still is moving, keeping his eyes trained on one patch of nervous water 90 feet in front of us.

Chuck says the hardest thing for fly-fishers to do is see redfish, because they are so busy looking at everything else around them. First, he wants to teach us all the things that *aren't* redfish, and then have us learn to ignore these countless distractions.

"Take your eyes and blur them across the horizon so you can ignore all the birds, mullet, and empty current, then start looking for water that stacks up, moves against itself, or just doesn't quite look right. It won't look like much at first, but believe me, all those humps are redfish."

Finally, the amateurs see the fish. One cast, two strips, and bang, a fish is on. Redfish are not picky eaters. Once they start rooting around with their heads in the grass, they munch in with blissful indiscretion. But they are hypersensitive to the underwater movements around them. Try as we might to steer this hooked fish away from the others, he splashes toward the school, and in a synchronized instant, the bottom of the pond jumps in a sudden surge. A muted drumming echoes over the

bay, as twenty decent reds charge out into the safety of the channel.

This place is done. We extract a mangled fly from the fish's crushers, make a photograph or two, and let him go, hoping that eventually, he, and we, might find the way back to the others. But now it is time to move on, Chuck says, and start over.

It seems like an elaborate operation, to measure the wind, the light and the tide-driven current, then maneuver yourself into position for one clean cast. If you are lucky or good, you can pick off cruising redfish one at a time. But a spooked school reshuffles the deck, and the guessing game begins anew. Every hour of every day, the redfish are on the move. We wonder how Chuck knows where to look for fish, and when to be there.

"You can't think of all the things that will change the patterns of these fish," he answers. "I came here thinking my biology degree might help, but after two weeks on the flats, I gave most of that textbook information up."

Most fishermen believe that redfish simply follow the movements of tide and

baitfish like clockwork, in and out of the south Texas labyrinth of tidal lakes, open bays, and estuaries on predictable daily schedules, but Chuck prefers to open his thinking to more complex, often incongruent, redfish hunting paradigms. The gravitational effects of the earth, moon, and sun, wind strength and direction, atmospheric pressure, and even intercoastal geography all combine to affect tidal range, duration, and velocity, which in turn, affect the movement of bait and redfish in varying degrees on any given day. Redfish, like most saltwater fish, like a lot of moving water and a lot of bait, but finding those perfect water conditions is not always as simple as it seems.

There are tidal charts and bait shop conversations that might help; Chuck has given up on those. There are times of bounty: New moon phases when the earth, moon, and sun are all in line (combining their gravitational pull), and tidal movement is heavy (*spring tides*), moving acres of bait, covering previously uncovered and fertile inlands, and putting redfish on the feed. There are times of scarcity: Quarter moon phases when the moon, earth, and sun form a right angle (weakening their gravitational pull), and tidal movement and range is dramatically reduced (*neap tides*), causing little or no flushing of bait, skinny flats water, and skittish, even sluggish, redfish. And there are the myriad of "in between" conditions that dominate Chuck's busy schedule.

"If you ignore traditional thinking, then this whole deal works," Chuck explains. "But it's all still just physics. When we get the water and bait we need, we should have fish, and they should be ready to eat. But you shut down that water movement, and we get real unhappy redfish."

"After you have been handed your hat and shown the door by Mother Nature a few times, you take off the blinders. Eventually, the smart angler embraces the 'Mother of All Axioms.' Everybody is partially right, and nobody is totally right. It is somewhere in the combined thinking where the truth lies."

Later that afternoon, Professor Naiser furthers our education on coastal Texas redfish culture with a short vocabulary lesson. Today's subject is the word "som-bytch" (Chuck spells it for our notes), which we

are told is usually a catch-all, anonymous noun, likely of East Texas origin, and particularly well-suited for describing both anglers and fish, or birds. It can be used in a masculine or gender-neutral context. It can, at times, be used as an exclamatory for effect, much like "ouch," or "dang." But it is important to note that *som-bytch*, is not necessarily a derogatory term; used properly, its function is merely to reflect or add emphasis to a preceding adjective, which when spoken, is naturally given extra inflection.

Chuck offers examples:

"After he got out of prison, he straightened himself out and was a *good* som-bytch."

"His chin was too small for his head, but he was a *smart* som-bytch."

"What are those *pink* som-bytches, are they flaminkees?"

"Look at that fish swim down the bank. Man, that is one *fast* som-bytch."

"He is dumber than a stump, but he's a *handsome* som-bytch."

Chuck smiles and ends the lesson by dropping the throttle and speeding off toward another spot. Enough culture, time to go fishing again.

"You get all that down?" he asks. An affirmative nod, still writing.

"Good. I could tell, you are an *astute* som-bytch."

Cary Marcus pulls his boat alongside ours, and tells Chuck the good news.

"There's fish in Paul's Mott—so many you could walk across their backs from one side to the other."

"Where are they?"

"In the east end, sandy side, past the second duck blind."

"To the right of the blind?"

"Yeah, to the right. You'll have to walk into them."

It was a relatively uncommon courtesy, and a nod of respect to Chuck. Cary could have stayed in the mott and pounded redfish until his arm was sore. Good friends share.

On the Texas coast, there are three ways to find the spots where the redfish concentrate. You can learn the hard way, through time on the water, which, says Chuck, is the best approach. You can depend on your friends to point you in the right direction. Or, you can bird-dog behind another guide and follow him. That is, if you trust he isn't

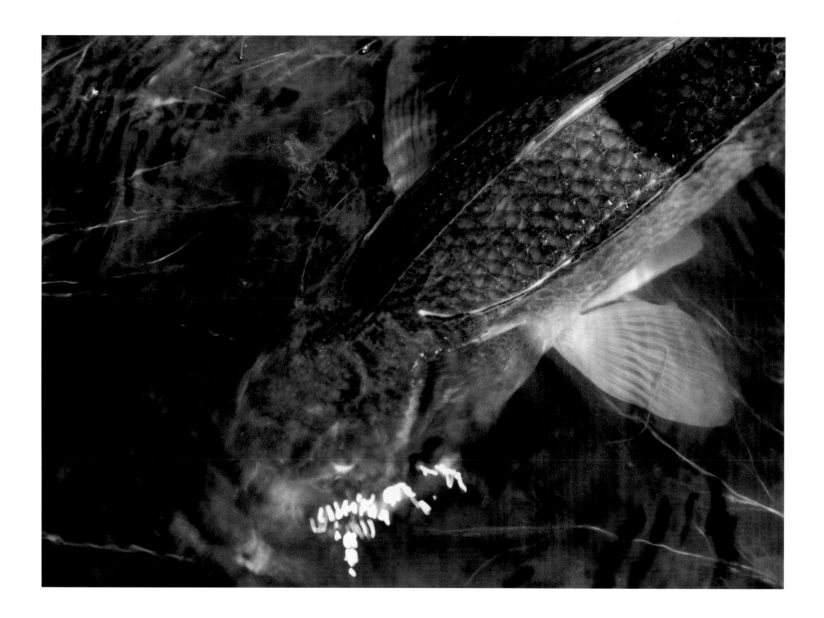

onto you, and you have a boat that can follow his.

It usually is not a good idea to chase Chuck Naiser. He is friendly enough with his information, but his "Curlew" boat is unlike anything we had ridden before. Wide and flat, its concave hull design sucks the water onto a protected surface-piercing prop, one that won't scar the bottom, but still allows the boat to motor through water that would wreck the average flats boat. Sliding through the marsh toward Paul's Mott, we are amazed as Chuck breaches standing grass and sandbars shrouded by a mere film of water. If anyone wanted to hang a hand over the side, they could scrape their knuckles on the bottom.

"She floats in 4½ inches, and runs where water used to be," Chuck shouts over the whirring engine.

"If anyone wants to follow me, I'll run 'em aground and say 'chase that'."

If it weren't for the wind, life would be perfect. We are knee deep on the sandy east edge of Paul's Mott, plodding forward, stepping quietly, and trying not to push a wake or make a splash. The breeze is up

now, blowing at about 20-knots. Chuck points at a fish about 80 feet away and says "go," but there is no cast, only a puzzled, intimidated look pointed back at Chuck.

"Look, you're going to have to make friends with the wind in Texas," he says. "Or you can come back in July, when it stops blowing for about 20 minutes, but that's when everyone's chasing down their chickens because they've been leaning so long in one direction that now they can't walk straight."

Point taken. Maybe it is time for a casting lesson.

Chuck explains that he made a choice long ago to live and die with the fly rod, and that meant learning how to cast in every possible condition. Do it right, and you will develop a "feel." Once you develop the feel, the fly rod will become the most dangerous redfish weapon on the flats. Chuck will stack his "buggy whip" against another person's "bubba stick" any day of the year.

Our minds play through Chuck's list of not-so-simple casting instructions: Rotate, follow through with the right hand over the left; a good cast is all in the hands; your left hand ends up on your pocket; when you false cast, keep your hands close together; when you let your hands fly apart, like you are playing an accordion, you take all the energy out of the rod; get the fly line up; know where the wind is—if it's off your shoulder, let it carry the line wide, if it's behind you, let the wind kite up under the line on the backcast, if it's in your face, let

the wind power your backcast; steady tempo; not too hard; if you want to shoot a gun further, you don't pull the trigger harder, do you?

Finally, 80 feet of fly line unfurls and drops a chartreuse Clouser exactly where the fish used to be. "That was perfect," Chuck says, already looking and walking toward the next fish.

"How could you tell?"

"You can always hear a perfect cast."

Look! Right up there, coming down the bank… see 'em?

"See what?"

"Two tails. Two big 'ol juicy tails!"

We creep into position to cut off the only escape to deep water, and wait for the redfish. They arrive on schedule, about a minute later, fins waving and fanning across the surface, refracting intense, white sunlight in random tangents. The first cast falls short. The second cast leads the fish by two feet. Pause, strip, bingo.

"He couldn't help it," Chuck laughs.

The redfish makes a nervous, full-on charge, pushing a wake on both sides, driving over the sand through very thin water,

high enough to expose the trademark black spot on his tail, flapping back and forth like a blinking eyeball. We turn the fish, and he runs back at us, forcing us to crank hard on the growling reel. Then he dashes again, and we let go.

In all, the fight lasts only a few minutes before the red tires, then burrows his head into the weeds. As we gather line, Chuck hollers over the walkie-talkie to Tim Clancey that we just "skinned the cat." They were both 28's, but this was the heavier of the two.

The fish is brilliant. Hues of red, pink, and copper run over in gentle contrast to the rich, green strands of wigeon grass. For the first time in a few days, Chuck is almost speechless.

He collects himself, then smiles.

"In the fall, when the wigeon grass lays down, I can pole back here, and the sun gets on these fish, and man, it's a beautiful sight. Those are days the reds sparkle like strawberries in a green field."

On the last day, as we speed north along the coast, auburn morning light streaks across the bays, and Chuck tells us we are headed to a special place, "where the old ones go to die, and God comes to visit."

We catch a few decent reds and a speckled trout for good measure, but mostly, we find ourselves absorbed by the expansive beauty of this Texas waterscape. We run out of jokes and stories, then we get thirsty. It is time to call it a trip.

We cap the day off with oyster baskets and a few cold beers at Pop's restaurant. The locals at the bar, in jeans and bent-brimmed baseball caps, ask Chuck how we did, but they already know. What we know is that we'll be headed back to South Texas, with its windy salt marshes, authentic food and character, and tailing redfish as often as we can, and it's a fair bet that Chuck will be there waiting when we do.

"Oh, I'll still be here doing whatever it is I do, and I hope it'll be for a long, long time, so long as the missus still thinks I'm workin'. When ya'll come back, I expect you to be better fishermen, 'cause I know I'll be," he laughs.

"We'll do our best. What do you think about next spring?"

"I think next spring sounds good."

"I'll call you," one of us promises.

"You do that. I'll be waitin'… darlin'."

Paul's Mott

You som-bytches might hightail it up on this flat

to have a look at these birds workin' redfish tailed-up

in wigeon grass, beautiful light coming through,

and I promise you won't find a prettier sight on this green earth.

Chuck, we've got magnums hazing rainbait in the grass—

just need one to put his head through the trees and see the fly.

Beautiful sight ain't it. *Oh, the good Lord*

has spent some quality time here in Paul's Mott, that's for certain.

Well, we just skinned the cat, took a twenty-eight and twenty-nine

comin' down the creekbed, and they were lit up like a couple of big red fire trucks.

Like rubies in a dirty pig's ass. We need to get you boys

out of that grass to some open water where he can set up some fish,

because these reds are half in the bag and ready to dance.

Chuck, I think he wants to stay and take his chances

with some of these stubborn magnums grazin' wigeon grass.

You tell that little darlin' not to waste all his energy

where there's no use puttin' it, and get up here and have at it.

Chuck, he just hooked a magnum, so we're all smiles now.

You tell that little darlin' that's not half-assed bad.

Oh, I think he's comin' around to our south Texas reds.

The good Lord always takes his time. *Amen.*

Amanda Switzer
East Hampton, New York

Amanda Switzer had left the door to her house unlocked. Phoning from her boat, she gives us directions to her quiet, oceanside street from East Hampton, tells us to let ourselves in, and not to mind Marlowe, her 13-year old yellow Lab. He is friendly. She will be off the water in another hour or two.

By this time, after a flight, a drive, a ferry ride, another drive, and another ferry, we all are in need of our own space. We spread out, one kicking back on the deck to read through notes, another grabbing the couch for a power nap, and the other futzing with the stereo in her kitchen, cueing up the CD in the rack. It is Depeche Mode.

Her phone rings, and the answering machine picks up. We feel awkward, because the volume is cranked up loud enough to broadcast the caller's message throughout the house. It is not like we want to eavesdrop on sister talk, a boyfriend, or business, but it is too late.

"Hi Amanda, it's A___. I found a few fish in Gardiners today. Call me and I'll fill you in. Bye." Then another call five minutes later: "Hey, it's P___. I had a pretty good day, starting to see some fish move into the flats by Sammy's. I'll call back later." Three more calls, all reports, or inquiries, all in captain-talk, about fish locations, water conditions, wind, and tide. We had read how this little community of fishing guides on the eastern end of Long Island—a veritable striped bass *La Cosa Nostra*—interacts by ritually trading or guarding secrets, offering advice, and making day-to-day plans, but this was our inadvertent introduction to how the system worked in real time.

We exchange sheepish glances when Amanda comes bounding up the stairs, skipping through abbreviated introductions on her way to change clothes. Returning, she puts her own plan in gear, asking us if we feel like fishing a little this evening. We say we're up for it.

"Great, you can cast can't you?" she asks, without trying to hide her true motive. We nod. "Okay, then let's go. There were fish all over the place today, but we couldn't get into them. I want to see if I was doing something wrong, or if that guy [her client] just sucked."

Amanda poles her 20-foot Hewes skiff along the lea shore of Shelter Island. The scene is not what we had envisioned. A dark canopy of mature, deciduous trees reflects off the surface of Smith Cove, white-tailed deer tip-toe around creek mouths, and shorebirds pick bait from the glacier-polished stones piled along the shoreline. In the evening, this bay looks like a quiet lake in the Catskills, or the rocky Wisconsin side of Lake Michigan.

"There's a bass at two o'clock, moving right, 20 feet from the shoreline," she says, cutting straight through the tranquility.

"That's 100 feet away."

"Go, go, go!" she shouts. "The bottom is dropping off, and I can't hold us here with the push pole!" The first cast falls woefully short. Voices of encouragement echo from the others in the boat: "You can do it, relax, we've seen you make that cast before." Amanda is not as patient. "What are you doing, he's moving away! Go again!" Another cast, certainly a respectable effort, but still 10 feet short. "C'mon, let's make a cast," she says.

Stripping the line back to prepare for another seemingly futile shot, the angler feels a second, unnoticed striper grab the fly and muscle toward the mouth of the bay. The fight is tough, bullish, and abrupt. We land the fish, admire its sculpted-green head and bright, chrome flanks evenly raked from gills to tail with black lateral lines. Amanda lets it go.

Before conceding "all's well that ends well," the angler and Amanda trade pointed glances from bow and stern, as if to mark their boundaries, and say without words, "so this is how it's going to be." Underlying the tension is the fact that, had she been doing the fishing, she would have made the cast to

the first fish on the first try, and everyone on the boat knows it.

For one slight moment, it seems as if she might throw down the push pole, he might drop the rod, and they might meet in the middle of the deck to start slugging it out, or else hug each other, but nobody knows for sure which way it would go.

Amanda rifles through piles of empty Diet Coke cans in the storage bin and cooler, finds a lukewarm soda, pops the top, takes a few gulps, and explains, almost apologetically, "I don't really yell at people on the boat. I just get excited." Captain Switzer is as complex, ironic, and ultimately compelling as the waterline. Her enthusiasm is genuine and her skill remarkable, yet she does not seem to know how really good she is. We are not sure we want to tell her.

On the one hand, there is an almost manic, New York-bred passion and intensity that drives Amanda; on the other, she exudes an uncommon grace and calm, an instinctive connection with things natural or unspoiled. Amanda is the only captain we ever have met to describe fishing as "stressful, but fun." She is artistic, but also techni-cal and pragmatic. She is independent, but relies on her family and close circle of friends for daily support. She is stern, but also giving. Her heart undoubtedly is kind.

She recalls how she learned to fish on the South Fork of Long Island, tagging along with old surfcasters who were fascinated by a young girl's lack of squeamishness with the bloody, daily business of baiting eels and menhaden, unhooking fluke and sea robins, and gutting bass and bluefish. Although side-tracked by "boys, beer, and bad haircuts" during her late teens, she would earn a college degree in environmental sciences, start her own landscaping business in 1991, and begin working offshore tuna and shark charters on the *Running Wild* in her spare time. After a three-year stint in New York City, earning another degree in landscape architecture, she finally decided that it was the right time to make the jump from angler to fly-fishing guide.

So in 1999, she scaled back her landscaping business, moved to East Hampton, and decided to become a captain. Amanda credits local fishing legend Paul Dixon for taking her under his wing (running charters from his overflow), and helping prepare her to

Amanda Switzer

compete and survive in the traditionally male-dominated world of inshore fly-fishing. Although they had met many years earlier, when Paul owned and operated an Orvis fly shop in East Hampton, she says Paul hired her because she "convinced him that [she] wouldn't let him down."

"Paul told me it was going to be a lot of hard work, with a very limited amount of financial rewards. He said most of the guides here supplement their income by having another career, and the ones that don't work elsewhere have financial backing, either with trust funds or a *very* supportive spouse. But the lack of money was a loss I was willing to take. The thought of being the only female sight-fishing guide in New York was something that I couldn't say no to, even if I had to do it for free."

The next morning we awake, on Amanda's command, at some ungodly pre-dawn hour. Word from the guide grapevine is that the stripers are congregated and feeding at Barcelona Point, early, when the falling tide flushes out bunker and eels from Northwest Creek. It should make for some nice beach casting.

There are no pre-set striped bass fishing rituals on this part of Long Island. The guides follow the fish, which follow the moon phases, weather, tides, and the bait. If the morning bite is going to happen at 4:30 a.m., so be it. The people who want to catch fish drag themselves out of bed and show up. The late sleepers get blanked.

Amanda stops briefly at the boat slip to pick up some gear, but somebody has ransacked her skiff and stolen her fly boxes. She launches into a brief, though subdued, tirade, whispering f-bombs under her breath so as not to wake the neighbors. Ultimately resigned to sadness and disappointment, she outwardly wonders why somebody would do something like that, "Why would anybody steal my flies? I spent all winter tying those, and I'm pretty sure I haven't pissed off anybody lately." We head back for home, and her fly bench, so she quickly can tie up some Clousers before we miss the outgoing tide and feeding stripers.

The road to the point twists along a golf course, then becomes a muddy, two-track trail through the woods. She makes a wrong turn. The rods tied to the roof rack scrape and bend nervously under hanging branches as we side-axle around deep puddles. Close enough, she says, we'll walk from here. Scaling down a steep dune scattered with sticker bushes, glacial moraine, and dense patches of poison ivy, we finally reach the shoreline.

A lone angler is casting flies into the bight, his silhouette outlined by rays of sunrise reflecting in low angles off Northwest Harbor. It is her fishing friend Ron. She tells him about having her flies stolen, and without hesitation, he sets down his fly rod, walks over to his truck, and hands her a dozen striper patterns. Amanda ties one on and starts casting from a spot 20 feet behind us, immediately connecting on a small striper.

"Sorry guys. I'll have to fish the frustration out of my system," she says. Bending down to release the bass, she looks over and smiles. "I feel better now. Don't worry, everything's gonna be okay."

Later that same afternoon, more rested and with her skiff put back together, Amanda decides to make a short run toward Sammy's Beach. In late spring, the stripers cruise the South Fork shorelines and extended shallows hunting spearing, crabs, and sand eels. If you work carefully, and avoid clunking the push pole on the rocky bottom, you often can slip up on loners or pairs, cruising over the mottled flats and dark green drop-offs.

She swings the boat next to a fish trap, kills the engine, and climbs onto the platform. She notices another flats boat, maybe a half mile away, running the next fish trap along the beach, then slowing to fish. "Hand me my cell phone will you?" she asks. She hits autodial and tucks the pole under her arm to hold the boat in place.

"Hey, it's Amanda… Yeah, I'm fine… How are you doing? Hey, are you fishing Sammy's? Yeah… I was just wondering if that was *you* who just cut me off on this flat." The voice in the phone grows louder, still muffled beyond our abilities to make out what he is saying, but clearly more animated than before.

She cuts back in. "I know you went far down the beach, but you still cut me off… Look, you could tell I was working in that direction… yeah, but which way is the boat pointed? No, which way am I pointed? It's okay, I'm not mad… No, I'm not chewing

you out… No, I'm just saying, the normal protocol is to come in behind someone if you want to work the same flat… No, I'm just *saying*, usual protocol is… Don't worry about it, we're moving anyway. I'll see you later. Bye."

With that, Amanda jumps off the platform, tosses the phone on the console, and tells us to crank up the rods. This flat is shot. The amended plan is to head back toward Shelter Island, maybe find some bluefish.

The afternoon air still is unsettled, as if summer is trying to take hold of the water and the land, without spring letting go. We feel this seasonal hand lock as the boat rips across the surface of Gardiners Bay, bouncing through walls of hot, land-driven air, then frothy, cooler patches carried in with the offshore winds.

A flock of least terns and herring gulls tracks over the east portal of Shelter Island Sound, marking a marauding school of bluefish eating their way through shoals of menhaden.

Amanda says when bluefish crash menhaden, they leave an oily slick in the water, and a sweet odor hanging in the air. It

smells like fresh-cut watermelon. She ties on yellow foam poppers and small sections of wire leader before we make random casts from both sides of the boat. Her only concern is that our flies push noticeable wakes, thus attracting the attention of the reckless, slate-colored school. All she has to do is keep the boat near the birds and bait, while we cast away, and the blues will take care of the rest.

Though less desirable as table fare than the striped bass, because of their oily, darkish meat, the bluefish is a respectable, tough-nosed fish, underrated by some, but admired by most for their fighting moxie and impressive rows of serrated teeth. At the moment, we are catching two-pound blues, or "cocktail blues," which Amanda thinks are "kinda cute." The late summer "choppers," fish from five to ten pounds, and the fall "slammers" or "alligators," fish over ten pounds, will give the angler all they can handle, she says, wrapping knuckles on screaming reels, mangling flies, and cutting through leaders.

"Just look at this school of blues we've found, jumping and flopping over the surface like a bunch of little Muppets. A couple

of hours ago, when we got run off Sammy's, I would've told you that our day was shot, but as a captain, you always have to keep pushing ahead, and make the best of bad of bad situation. I've always felt that the greatest rewards in life come to you at unexpected moments."

Anyone who knows anything about East Coast striper fishing has heard about the "fall blitz" off the east end of Long Island. Every year, like herds of buffalo moving south along the plains, thousands and thousands and thousands of striped bass, bluefish, weakfish, tuna, herring, menhaden, anchovies, and the birds that follow them run en masse down the Atlantic Coast, driven by cooling New England waters, seasonal spawning urges, and the complex, interrelated effects of both the gulf and jet streams. Ideally, strong currents and changes in water temperature stall herds of bait in the waters near Montauk Point, and congregate untold numbers of gamefish. The result can be weeks of albacore, bluefish, and striped bass feeding frenzies.

The blitz often begins in mid September, and, in some years, runs past

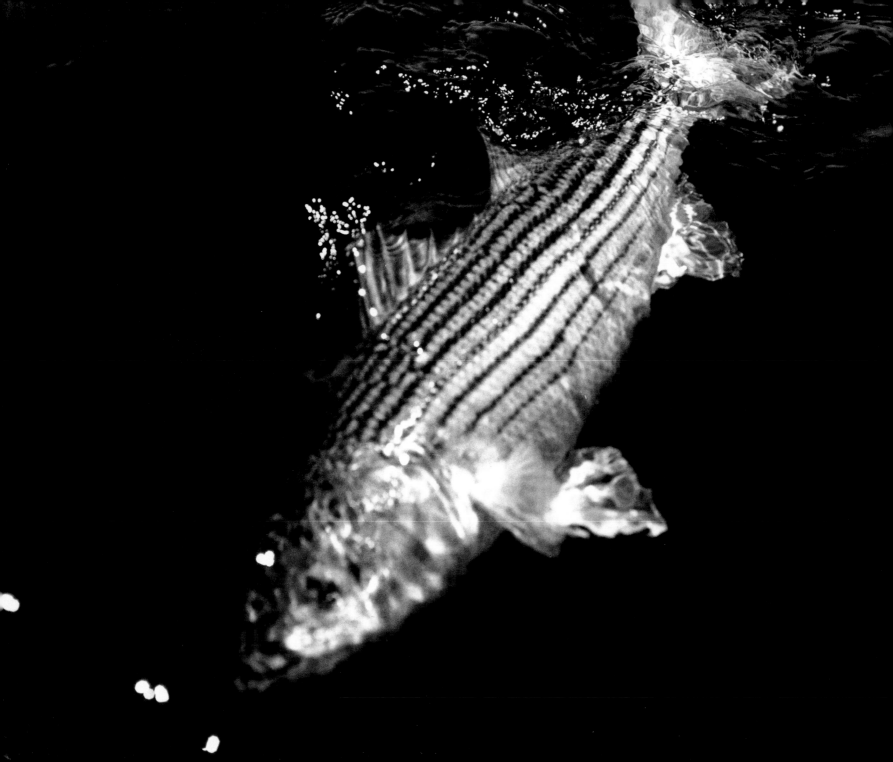

Halloween into November (given a late herring run), though you never can plan with certainty when the phenomenon will begin or end. Some people migrate out to the Island's east end with overstuffed cars and RVs, camping out and waiting for the one moment when the sea, weather, bait, and tons of stripers line up and come alive.

The fly-fishing captains, Amanda included, already are here in early September, running larger boats through the rips and shoals around Shagwong and Montauk Points, burning more gas, working the phones, and scouting for early signs of the impending chaos.

"You have to see the blitz to believe it," says Amanda. "Just the sight of the ocean working like that is an experience no one could forget. There are times when we're surrounded by so many gorging stripers that you can't hear yourself speak over the deafening sound. You wonder how all these fish got here, and where they came from."

Amanda, however, had chosen June for our fishing adventures, not that she was holding out on us, but she prefers this time of year for the difficult, sight fishing challenges of the flats.

"From a technical standpoint, guiding the fall blitz can be like driving a bus," explains Amanda. "There's something much more primal about seeing fish in close, and sneaking up on them. I'm not sure fishing the blitz can ever give you that feeling."

Afternoon showers blow us off the water. We stop at the old fish factory and grab some fresh lobsters to boil for dinner. Sitting around the kitchen counter that night, Amanda explains how, when all the stripers, false albacore, and bluefish run south down the Atlantic Coast, marking the end of another fishing season, she usually takes off for somewhere warm. This year, she does not know where she will end up.

By her own admission, Amanda has an angler's wanderlust. It is a difficult problem when you find yourself constantly tempted by remote pieces of water and that next fish species to be found thousands of miles away. When you are home, you think about all the far away places you would rather be, she says, but out on the road, you wonder about your family and friends, and miss the simple, private comforts of home. Never really knowing where you are going or where you belong is, at once, the most exciting and most disheartening part of the equation. We understand.

To her credit, Amanda has acted on more wanderlust impulses than most ever dare. She often hosts destination trips for the "Urban Angler" with friends like Dixon or on her own. Her travels have taken her to Nicaragua, Belize, Panama, Costa Rica, Honduras, New Zealand, Alaska, the Seychelles, throughout the Caribbean and South America.

"I'm thinking I'll head down to Mexico and catch some bonefish," she says, dunking a claw into the community pot of drawn butter. "A bonefish could pull a trout around the world backwards, and after that, it might have to be a tarpon or permit in the Keys. Next to striped bass, tarpon are my favorites."

She also is considering staying close to home, reaching out in new directions. She talks about writing a memoir on fishing, and even a children's book. This spring, she wants to host a camp for teenagers, teaching environmental ethics and fisheries preservation. The dinner talk ultimately resolves nothing,

but we know that if and when Amanda gets to that place where she is wandering, she will like it there.

On the last morning, she hands off the push pole. The stupid one accepts this as a challenge and learning opportunity; the obsessed, obstinate partner insists on fishing more; the photographer has seen enough wind and rain, and is headed home.

"The perfect man cooks *and* poles a boat. You guys had better learn that now," she says.

Amanda curls up on the seat cushion behind the wheel, pulls her baseball cap down over her eyes, rolls her jacket into a pillow, and tells us to wake her up if we catch anything big. We work the north shoreline of Hog Creek, in and among the docks and moored pleasure boats, even coaxing a few schoolie stripers to a small, white streamer. It is not much more than catching sunnies in a millpond, but we get a sense of satisfaction from pulling off this stunt on our own. Hey, we're striper fishing!

Swinging the push pole over the deck to reposition the skiff, we inadvertently splash water on Amanda's ballcap and face.

"Do that again and I'll get up and shove you off the back of the boat, and you can swim home," she whispers, eyes still closed.

The wind is kicking again from the east. Pushing home is easier said than done, but we make it, and at that, call an end to this East Coast striped bass adventure. Pulling into her driveway, she offers one final, candid thought,

"You know what guys? I'm not any good at math, I can't tell a decent joke, and I can be horrible when it comes to maintaining relationships, but the one thing I am good at is fishing. Without the sea, my life would be a desert."

Amanda drives us to the train station, and we say goodbye. She offers to show us a Montauk bass blitz later this fall if we have the time, but knows we will be busy with the book. She hopes we found the east end's stripers and bluefish as beautiful and interesting as she believes they are. She even is mildly upset, now that she thinks about it, that we did not see an iridescent albacore, but it is time to buy train tickets and head home.

Riding the Long Island Railroad, first past polo fields and estates, then through suburbia, and finally among the rows and rows of decrepit projects, we are struck by how quickly the world and the environment can change in a few hours, or a hundred miles, especially in New York. We had woken up to challenge the pristine and natural, and now we were deep in the heart of the urban hustle and grind.

After a change at Jamaica station, we are standing outside Penn Station, waiting in line at the taxi stand with fly rods slung over our shoulders. Windblown, tired, and trying to shake out a soppy pair of deck shoes and shorts, we look, we are sure, like the proverbial fish out of water. Then we think of something Amanda said a few days earlier.

"No matter where you are, or what you're doing at the time, the only constant is you. All these fish, and people, and places, come and go, but in the end, it's about what makes you keep going, or keep looking for something different. I think the journey is the story. That might be as good as it gets."

Barcelona Point

Up at four-thirty in the morning to fish
the last of the pitch-black striper bite at Barcelona Point,
a narrow bottleneck of puma-colored sand, broken whelks, and faded scallops
between Northwest Creek and the harbor, where glass minnows
and baby bunker pour out on falling tide to runaway
gangs of bass and bluefish, where you can stand at sunup
and take fish on every cast when they are in.

When bluefish and bass tear through schools
of bunker our Captain says it smells like watermelon in the wind
(she has Posey smell), but this morning, we missed the bite.
Our effort has produced a bass small enough
to fit in your hand—ten inches of South Fork striper
with seven lateral stripes like black wagon tracks across a mercury prairie;
from its dark green back stab ragged spines, whittled like fence posts.

An osprey, three black skimmers raking krill,
and a dozen least terns falling like stones from the sky into the sea;
the birds are the last farmers of the Island's eastern plains;
the sea the only true prairie left in East Hampton.
Beyond the horizon, party boats stack enormous sow bass
like cordwood, trawlers drag up the ocean floor,
and no one can stop the heavy, industrial machinery of New Jersey.

Steve "Creature" Coulter

Hatteras, North Carolina

Creature says he never has seen so much ugly green water in his life.

We hear the tuna bite is on, but it's a far run, maybe 40 miles, north and east of Hatteras. We can save that for tomorrow if the reports are still good. June isn't tuna time anyway. Creature just wants to "get us on base" with some dolphins on the fly.

The Estonian girl behind the counter fixes us some Johnny Bucks, Creature's favorite breakfast sandwiches, then we head over to the boat. It is almost sunup, and Dave Chambers, the ship's mate, is waiting on the *Sea Creature*, snipping mackerel and butterfish into chum. He has worked with "Creach" for five years, enough time to know the system as instinct. He works quietly, like an acolyte tending to his solemn business before mass.

The twin diesels rumble to life, we cast off, slip out into Pamlico Sound, round the inlet, and Creature points her out to sea. It is unusually calm and hot. Not a puff of wind. Running this inlet on a rough day, you can knock your teeth out on the wheel, or worse. The average Hatteras day will bang you around pretty hard, and have you holding on to something sturdy almost all the time. Today, it is no more than driving over a few speed bumps in a parking lot. We're lucky, but maybe not with the fishing.

"If we can find us some pretty water, we ought to be okay," says Creature. "I know we'll get into some dolphins. We might even jump a sail or a white marlin.

"And you never know… we might just hook a blue one."

Creature is a captain, not a fishing guide, and the differences are more profound than a Coast Guard license or an expensive, offshore boat. In Creature's case, it means he straddles the gray area between sport charters and commercial fishing, a bloodier, and often more dangerous business entirely.

Eighty percent of his summer work is running charters to fill the coolers and freezers of vacationing day trippers; in winter, after the schools of bluefin and yellowfin tuna pour back into the Hatteras banks, what's left of his season becomes about the market, money, and fish buyers.

"When people ask me what I do for a living, I say I kill fish."

Yet Creature has a unique affinity for the chase, the release, and the sport associated with pelagic fly-fishing. He is the man the glory seekers call when they want to chase world record tuna in November, when unruly seas have anglers looking *up* at the fish swimming through swells, and in the hospital afterward to fix violent seasickness.

In Captain Coulter, there is a gentile, quiet persona that somewhat defies the "Creature" moniker—a true southern gentleman, polite, good natured, sharp and cagey, and most interestingly, a man who seems to have found a working niche on the Atlantic Coast's ragged edge.

We are not surprised to learn that

Creature has a soft spot in his heart for the fly-fishermen. He never chastises the trout bum. He is one himself. Creature has been to Lees Ferry, and every year visits western Montana. He told us about the time he once was working a Montana river with an Elk Hair Caddis, when a 22-inch rainbow jumped out of a run and grabbed his fly before it ever hit the water. Throughout the battle, Creature kept asking his trout guide, over and over, if they could keep the fish, but once it was landed, Creature gently slipped the trout back into the water without saying a word.

"You didn't want to kill that fish after all, did you?" the guide asked.

"No sir. But I hear that so much every day as a charter captain, I just wanted to put it back on someone else for a change."

Fly-fishing in the open ocean is an odd contradiction, one that leaves you feeling a bit like you have brought a knife to a gunfight. As we roar east into the sunrise, watching the land behind us fade into a gray sliver, eventually vanishing altogether, we wonder how we are going to find fish in these open miles of nothing.

Creature smiles, lights a cigarette, and starts to explain.

He says it is all about changes. Changes in water, changes in currents, changes in structure (on the sea floor or on the surface), like weed mats, debris, and so on. Fish like changes. Find the change, and you find the bait. Find the bait and you find the fish. Simple.

"This is a screwy day. Nothing's lining up. Everything's cocked sideways. But usually, it's not a whole lot different than your trout fishing," he says. "You're looking for changes in the river, changes in the currents, and changes in the bottom."

We aren't buying it.

"Only we have a *whole* lot more water."

He goes on to describe the Atlantic Ocean's vast tapestry of varicolored currents: Ugly green water, pretty green water, pretty blue water, purple water, blended water, and so on, each intricate variation the complex result of intermixing different amounts of algae, sediment, light, temperature, weather, and the powerful gulf stream. Staring over the edge of the *Sea Creature*, we wonder to ourselves, "What's the color of *that* water?"

"Still ugly green," Creature remarks, without being asked.

"How can we tell what water is what?"

"You just will. Before you leave here, you'll know. You'll get to tell just by looking."

"How will we know pretty blue water when we see it?"

"You'll know pretty blue water because all blue water is pretty."

"Crank 'em up, Dave, we're moving." Over the radio, another charter captain says he has some dolphins under eel grass.

We run hard for a few minutes, then sidle up next to another boat. The dolphin (Creature calls them dolphin; further south, it's dorado, and in the grocery, mahi mahi) are slashing and diving through the prop wash like electric charges lit up with adrenaline.

Creature idles the engine, and tells us to grab a fly rod. Dave throws a handful of chum behind the boat to exaggerate the feed. A short cast, a few strips with a small baitfish pattern, and a hook up. The fish goes airborne with a violent shimmer, and

almost jumps in the boat. Another jump, and another, and finally, the jumping green fish pops off.

"These are just bailers anyway," Creature shouts down with a laugh.

On the *Sea Creature*, dolphin come in two sizes, bailers and gaffers: Bailers, about two feet or less, are dolphin you scoop into the boat, pop the fly, then throw back into the sea to swim another day; gaffers are bigger fish, which you fight to the transom, where the mate reaches over and impales with a sharp instrument, and then in one straining motion, flops into the ice box. Dave finishes the operation by sitting on the cooler lid as the fish does its death flap, sounding, at a distance, like nails being driven erratically into linoleum.

We hook 15 or 20 bailers, and one nice bull gaffer, before they start to slow down. Roundhouse sweeps with the fly try to coax up one last fish, but all at once, they're gone. Creature decides it is time to drop the teasers and troll some more, but almost everyone is played out. Tomorrow, he says we'll try something different, maybe chase after those tunas.

"Well, we took care of that business.

Maybe we'll have to up the ante in the morning," Creature says.

Cumulous clouds boil up on the horizon, indicating Lands' End. Nothing serious. It won't storm tonight, but the wind will start shifting to the south as this front moves by. The seas will be up tomorrow.

We ask Creature what he does when he gets stuck in a lighting storm.

"Well, your first choice is to steer around 'em altogether." Then he reaches into the gear box and pulls out a pair of insulated electrical lineman's gloves. "You can also wear these. They're good for up to 5,000 volts."

Now everyone on the boat understands that lighting packs a hell of a lot more punch than 5,000 volts, which begs the question, what do you do when the voltage surpasses glove strength?

"When it looks *real* bad, the best thing to do is let the mate drive."

Dave pokes his head up through the ladder hole with raised eyebrows.

Dave has been working with Creature for five years. They parted ways for a few months in the spring, but Dave came back, and Creature welcomed him. Like any good partnership, they have disagreements, feel at times like they need their own space, but ultimately, realize that the right hand is better with the left, and vice versa.

Dave is as good a mate as they come. He's funny. He smiles. He tells you you're doing a good job in the heat of a fish battle (which boosts morale), and quietly fixes your screwups when you are looking the other way. He can rig ballyhoo teasers as the boat is ripping through very rough water, and it's all you can do to stay vertical. Dave and Creature communicate without words, they anticipate each other's next move, and they respect each other immensely.

The bridge, the wheel, and the boat may belong to Creature, but the deck, where most of the fishing action unfolds, belongs to his mate. He sets the baits and teasers, pays out the line, rigs the flies, keeps the matrix of fishing lines untangled, and he's the guy who will grab, without hesitation, that leader when the fish is thrashing behind the transom.

It doesn't take long to realize that your mate is doing most of the *real* fishing, and

you're just there for the cast, the hook set, the cranking of the reel, and in the end, a pretty photograph. The fact that most fishermen aren't seriously injured, or that the on-deck chaos somehow finds order, is a testament to the mate's quiet but backbreaking work. Without him, no one on the *Sea Creature* would catch a fish.

On day two, we are out on the new moon. The red sun is on the rise, and winds will blow at 10 knots from the south. We still are lucky by Hatteras standards.

Sailors appropriately coined the phrase, "the Graveyard of the Atlantic" for Cape Hatteras, because this water has seen over 1,000 shipwrecks since the 1600s. Known as one of the harshest, most dangerous stretches of ocean on the east coast, Diamond Shoals, a 12-mile long sandbar, is the meeting place for two of the ocean's strongest currents—the northbound gulf stream and the cold Labrador current running south along the coast. The resulting collision rapidly changes the shape of the sandbars into shifting, erratic patterns on the relatively shallow bottom. Over the years, sailors and authors have described surf, sand, and shells literally exploding into the air as a result of this encounter.

We aren't far from the wreck of the *USS Monitor*, one of the most famous ships claimed by the Cape. The ship survived a battle against the *CSS Virginia* and spent nearly a year in the treacherous waters off Cape Hatteras guarding the harbor. Considered "unsinkable," the *Monitor* took a turn for the worse when she could not withstand the force of Diamond Shoals and sunk to the bottom. At that time, it was a wreck comparable to the sinking of the *Titanic*. Wreck searchers didn't find her broken hull for almost 100 years.

Running up the coast, we notice the landmark candy-striped lighthouse, which is actually the third lighthouse attempt for Hatteras. The need for a light to reach 20 miles off the coast to warn wary sailors from the dangers of Diamond Shoals precipitated a need for the tallest lighthouse in the United States. Cape Hatteras lighthouse is 208-feet tall. Despite the lighthouses' presence, several wrecks, such as the *Huron* and the *Iron Steamer*, still are visible from the shore.

Creature has decided to make the long

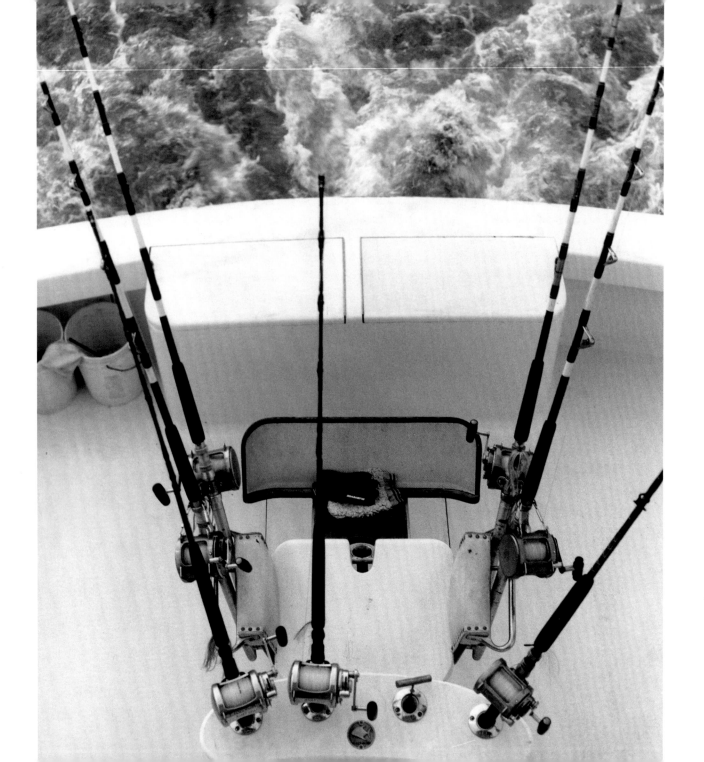

run northeast to find the tuna bite because there are no guarantees these yellowfins will hang around any longer. He thinks the tuna will follow the cooler water further up the Carolina shoreline. He also thinks this might be our last, best shot to take a yellowfin on a fly, at least until fall.

Yet, if conditions turn, Creature won't tempt fate, and he won't tempt the Cape. He knows the limits of his boat, and himself, and you can be certain both are a lot higher than yours.

"When I say it's time to head in because of the weather," explains Creature. "We're heading in."

Fall is when the tunas return en masse to the Outer Banks to blitz on mackerel and other baitfish, ripping through schools of bait with such ferocity that even the "sporty" fly-rodder has a good chance of tossing an artificial into the mix and coming up with a respectable fish. It is the one time of year you can shoot the fishing dice and know you'll see sixes and eights, the hard way, on a fairly consistent basis, so long as you have the will to fight the cold wind, icy rains, and waves.

June, on the other hand, is a mixed bag, and certainly not prime time for tuna on the fly. The radio chatter goes on:

"Ain't no way you're gonna get a tuna to eat a fly today…you can fill that box in an hour the regular way, but they ain't gonna eat no damn fly." Even Creature hedges his bets. Maybe we will, maybe we won't.

We fall asleep, despite the roar of the engines and the lurches *Sea Creature* makes as it rumbles over the backsides of swells.

An hour later, Dave wakes the angler by kicking his foot. Wiping the haze from our eyes and stepping onto the deck, we see the armada in the faint morning light. It is a surreal scene. After the long run through nothing but slate gray isolation, there are 30 boats, green sticks, commercial vessels, party boats, and private charters, all running in even patterns over a common point on the GPS, like riding mowers making even sweeps across an enormous water field.

Dave says to rig up. We wonder which rod for a moment, but soon notice that Creature only is working a half-spread. We are going fly-fishing.

Now, cruising into that bunch of boats with one rigger up is more than tying a

hand behind your back. It is like flying a pirate flag, declaring war on the windmill, and charging headlong into the mix with a middle finger raised for all the other charter captains who said we couldn't catch a tuna on the fly.

"Get them teasers in the water, Dave," Creature yells as he drops the boat to a troll. Then he shouts at us: "Get that line payed out and laid on the deck. There're tuna all over the place."

The first yellowfin eats a dead bait on a conventional rod. Dave plays him near the transom with the rod in his left hand, then tosses a few butterfish off the back with his right, trying to "chunk up" the rest of the school where the angler can make a short cast. But this school passes, then evaporates into unlit water.

"Dag-gonnit," Creature shouts. "Put him in the box, Dave. Let's go find us some tuna that'll eat a fly."

Dave gaffs the tuna, drops him in the box, slams the lid shut, and we start over. Twenty minutes later, another yellowfin eats the rigged ballyhoo, and we're back in business. Dark blue shadows swirl behind the transom. We watch the white Puglisi fly sink toward oblivion, and suddenly disappear in a navy blue shadow. It's a hard take.

Three jabs to the side, and then let go. Listen to the reel music. He first runs out, then down. Straight down.

Creature cheers. "Atta boy. Hang on to him, he's a nice one." The rest of the school jumps and slashes at another handful of butterfish Dave tosses over, just for grins. We have enough to worry about now.

"They're rolling in the chum, boys, they're rolling in the chum!"

Minutes seem like hours, and the sweat pours as the fisherman strains just inside the breaking point of an 11-weight fly rod. Eventually we see the football-shaped fish silhouetted in the depths off the stern, working a death dance, swimming in slow, even, counterclockwise spirals.

Ten circles, maybe 12, and the tuna breaks the surface. Dave is there with the gaff, and the 45-pound tuna goes from living thing to dinner fare, just like that.

"That's how we do it boys," Creature grins, as he kicks the boat back in gear. "Get that daisy-chain back in the water, and we'll do it again."

Steve Coulter

On day three, the wind shifts further southeast, pushing the swells to four feet or better. We have the story in the can. This day is for fun. We're going to take a longshot gamble, with a full-spread and conventional tackle, and go looking for a marlin.

Creature is on the bridge. Dave has the stereo pumping out Bob Marley, and watches the spread, making sure the ballyhoo teasers are swimming, not twisting.

"Check that right flat," Creature shouts. Dave is already on it.

We are in 1000 fathoms. It is pretty blue water. We can tell now. We've run just far enough, maybe 30 miles, to catch the edge of the gulf stream. The water is 83.4 degrees. The current is strong enough to undercut the waves and knock them down by a foot or more. We are rocking into a light sleep, when at once, all hell breaks loose.

"On the long line! Your side, Dave!"

"I got it!"

"It could be a blue one! Watch out there! Watch him!" He's running hard underneath.

Dave hands off the rod and clips the angler into the chair, then spins around to crank in the other rods. Creature reels in the teasers on the outriggers and drops the boat into neutral. There is a sudden, almost eerie silence, interrupted only by the sound of the water and the whir of line peeling off the reel.

Dave watches the reel, and bends over to listen. He says you know it's a blue one if

they grab it and start to accelerate, faster…
then faster… then faster.

"This might be… c'mon, baby… this
could be…" Dave whispers.

And then, he just smiles. He stands and
shouts over his shoulder at the bridge:

"Creach… it's *him*."

At days end we run back to Hatteras
Harbor with two small blue-and-white
marlin flags flying upside down, which
means we let two blue ones go. All we are
bringing back today is the silk on the string,
and nothing in the box for the picture takers at the marina.

The first marlin had run straight back
and cut a 90-degree angle before starting a
series of jumps off the starboard side of the
boat; the second—the big one—just held in
place, shaking her head back and forth, and
created a slick the size of a basketball court
with spray.

When we turned the second one loose,
Dave had to work fast, as the big blue marlin was coloring back up. Creature figured it
weighed 600 pounds. After Dave popped
the hook, we all watched her black, serrated
tail start waving as she dropped back down

into the Atlantic Ocean. The last time we
saw that fish, she was just a small, trout-like
shadow under the stern.

"Hey Creach… pretty blue water,
right?"

"Yeah… pretty blue water."

We celebrate back at the marina with a
slash of wild cherry moonshine in the ice
room behind the tables of fish cutters.

Creature says a two-marlin day might
have fetched a year's worth of salary or
more in the Big Rock Tournament two
weeks ago. We were a little late. Yet had we
caught those fish then, they would have
been gaffed, dragged through the back door,
and now be hanging on the pole in the
boatyard. We sense that these magnificent
fish, not the money, are what keep Creature
and Dave grinding the long hours, burning
hundreds of gallons of diesel gas, and looking out over the sun-bleached horizon for
pretty blue water.

"That's why I'm a captain," says
Creature. "I marlin fish. It's too tough and
too unpredictable to do it every day. But
that one moment when you see a marlin on
your line, it'll change your life. You never
get over it."

Pretty Blue Water

Creature runs an hour through ugly greenwater,
pretty greenwater, ugly greenwater, pretty greenwater
until the symmetry evolves like grooves in a giant vinyl record
or the edges of torn current across Montana's Bitterroot River.
There is no such thing as ugly bluewater or purplewater
(deep, deep bluewater), because all bluewater or purplewater is pretty.
We won't look for either today. Dorado prefer
pretty greenwater and floating mats of sargasso for cover.
Creature says dolphin even shade themselves under
drifting garbage, plywood, turtles, or dead whales.
Dave, the ship's mate, drags teasers along weed mats, chums squid
and oily fish, then we all watch as fifty to a hundred
bailers and gaffers draft the afterwake like flocks
of electric green gulls swarming the embarcadero.

Rick Murphy
Homestead, Florida

In the Everglades, you can smell a good tarpon day when it is about to happen. There is a sweet early morning scent, the fragrance of lacy white flowers from Spanish stopper trees suspended in the humidity, woven through the mangroves and hanging over the flats. The smell is only there when the wind, moisture, and heat are right, and its presence is a sure harbinger that, when the tides move, the big fish will be rolling.

It is late July, hideously buggy, and a series of thunderheads tower like gray and black anvils above Florida Bay, bouncing soft strobes of light out and over the miles of dark, uneven water.

Standing at the Flamingo boat ramp, Rick Murphy is deciding whether he wants to fish "inside" or "outside." The professional redfish tour is in town. A handful of boat captains—the competition—waits in the staging area near the ramp, their silhouettes highlighted by the morning moonlight, distant lightning, and sporadic embers from their burning cigarettes. They think Murphy is going scouting.

A typical day in Flamingo offers many options. You can work the backcountry mangroves for snook, or cut out to the keys and basins, hoping to find redfish on the oyster bars and edges. Of course, you also can chase after bonefish on the sandy, turtle-grass flats.

But the first deep breath of humid morning air already had confirmed Rick's plan. We are going after tarpon. We will fish inside, he says, push Coot Bay, then through Whitewater Bay toward the northwest, and go as far as we have to, maybe as far as Shark River Island. This way, we can dodge the rain and lightning storms if we have to, and take advantage of the last two hours of a falling tide.

Murphy is on a mission.

"Oh, we'll get into some tarpon today," he says. "I can smell it. I'm not sure how we'll catch 'em, or where we'll catch 'em, but I'm not worried. Trust me."

Running north from Flamingo, through one of many channels cut by Flagler's barges, we emerge into a small bay obscured by a light morning mist and walled in with dense stands of dark green, almost black mangroves. The surface of the tannin water along the near east edge is ringed almost entirely with life, like a kettle of bubbling soup, indicating the presence of fish, massed in a disorganized school, maybe two acres long. It is a curious sight, more akin to trout gulping *callibaetis* on Hebgen Lake, than anything we had seen in warm water.

"Who wants to catch the first tarpon?"

"Tarpon?"

"Yeah, this is the nursery, the playpen. Grab that six-weight fly rod, and put on a small Clouser. We might as well teach them while they're young."

We pause before making our first casts, long enough to notice that these fish are playing out, in miniature, the same routine of the grownups, daisy-chaining in distinct circles, gulping air, and milling through the shadows in search of bait.

It only takes a few casts to iron out the kinks, and the small green and white streamer grabs the attention of a baby tarpon, who inhales it with hereditary vigor, and just like its bigger brethren, vaults straight into the air with a violent shimmer. We trade shots from the bow for an hour or so before three alligators drift nonchalantly into the mix, attracted by the distressed splashing and pretending as if we don't notice them, but not really caring if we do. When the largest gator, roughly six feet long, drifts to within 20 feet of the boat, Rick says it is time to take off and let things settle down.

"See, I told you we would have a 20 tarpon day!" he shouts. "Are we done? Did you get what you wanted?"

"Maybe not."

"Me neither, let's go find a big one."

Two large tarpon free jump on the west side of Oyster Bay. Rick kills the engine and climbs onto the poling platform. They're

in here, he says, so be patient. Whisper. Don't move your feet, and don't bump anything. Coil up the fly line on the deck. Hold the Cockroach in your hand. Don't bother blind casting in this stained water. The odds that your false casting and line commotion will hurt us outweigh the odds of teasing up one lonely, indiscriminate bite. We will wait until one rolls in close, then lead him with a cast, start stripping, and pray.

We see a player. The fish porpoises at 11 o'clock from the bow and is heading right, no more than fifty feet away, and almost close enough to count the hundreds of aluminum-to-green scales densely packed along its rolling flank and back.

When he eats the fly, the world changes in one second. What had been utter silence, except for the slicing whisper of a fly line overhead, explodes with the terrified, gill-rattling contortions of the tarpon going airborne. The fish jumps three, four times like successive, molten silver shots from a giant Roman candle, each time crashing lengthwise against the surface, sending echoes like cracking timber over the flat.

"Run Forrest…RUN!!" Rick laughs, as the fish charges at the mangrove shoreline.

It isn't a terribly large tarpon, maybe 60 pounds. Yet, he packs more than enough staying power and tenacity to humble the trout bum on the bow, who stammers a chain of epithets at himself and the tarpon, as his face turns red and his neck arteries bulge with the strain on the rod. Poor bastard, Rick says, he's ruined. He'll never be the same again. A tarpon will change a man's life forever.

"Breathe, man, don't forget to breathe," Rick instructs through a contented, "welcome to my world" grin.

For 20 minutes or more, the fish shows little quit, running in circles around the boat, warping the 11-weight rod near its breaking point, and shuffling the three of us around the deck in a Keystone Kops routine. Finally, Rick grabs his yellow tarpon gloves.

"Now go around the bow. The front. The *other* front," he says. "Okay, hang on, gimme that leader, we got him now."

For Rick Murphy, fly-fishing is a business, and he won't apologize for utilizing the sport as a way to earn a generous living for both himself and his family. You can resent him for his slick boats, his televi-

sion show (*Sportsman's Adventures with Captain Rick Murphy*, which airs on the Sunshine Network), his sponsorships, magazine covers, advertisements, and his house full of trophies won both as an angler on the pro redfish tour and as a winning fishing tournament guide, but in the end, he has learned how to make a living by doing something he loves, and it is hard to fault him for that.

His passion is genuine; his skill precise and apparent. After all, there are no "gimmes" on the Florida flats. Rick doesn't just talk the talk, he walks the walk, and after 10 minutes in his boat, even the most novice angler can figure that out.

"There are differences between going fishing, guiding, and making a career," says Rick. "Everyone should be allowed to take their passion and interest to whatever level they choose and are able, without all the politics and backstabbing, but that's all part of the game."

In Rick's case, it starts with his firebrand intensity, the likes of which none of us has ever encountered before. The atmosphere on the boat is always jovial, humorous, sometimes downright raunchy, but when it's money

time, Murphy calls the shots. "This is a war," says Rick, "and we're always on the offensive."

The man has been known to bite sharks, and tarpon fishing, where you try to find, hook, and land fish with the size and power of personal watercraft in 10 feet or less of water, he says, is not a finesse game, fly rod or not.

"When you hook that fish, you gotta fight him like you want to rip his face off," he explains. "He'd rip yours off if he could. You give the fish one break, you let yourself lose control, and he's gonna turn it on *you*.

"You gotta remember they think they're gonna die. For the tarpon it's always a fight to the death. They don't know we're gracious, and they don't expect mercy, so don't give them any until that last moment, when you look into that big black eye and decide to send 'em home."

Without his unrelenting intensity, it is hard to imagine that Rick Murphy could have achieved the fishing success in south Florida he has. Not only is flats guiding a technically difficult, physically demanding, and meager paying profession to break into, but a young, green entrepreneur also must find his niche in the thriving Keys and Everglades "old boy" network, where weathered veterans still guard flats like cattle barons fending off rustlers. This is hallowed water, and it *should* require more than a cell phone, a captain's license, and a flats boat to call yourself a Florida flats guide, but no one has any idea, says Rick, how truly difficult it is to break in down here.

Yet every season a fresh wave of young guns and displaced Yankees flock down to south Florida in droves, each figuring they have found tropical paradise, lots of fish, and a perfect place to hang a shingle. But Rick points out, it isn't the good ones, or the tough ones, who last. The captains who make it here are both good and tough, and natural selection usually sends the others packing.

Respect is the dividing line. Rick had mentors to teach him that—people like Stu Apte and Al Pflueger, Jr. Back in the 1970s when the sport really took off, the founding members of the Miami Sportfishing Club laid out an unwritten protocol for fishing and guiding—how much space you should give another boat on a flat, how to approach tailing or rolling fish without cutting off others, where to motor, where to pole, and

so on. Understanding and adhering to the protocol is the first step to survival, Rick says, but sometimes, the last test is being willing to stand your ground.

He explains how he once was crowded off a run full of tarpon by a well-known veteran, who knew full well how the system worked but wanted to flex some muscle and back Rick down. An uncomfortable shouting match was avoided on the water, but later that evening, Rick called the man to inform him he was standing on his boat with six gallons of gas and a lighter, and was ready to "go to work" if they didn't have a talk to sort things out. No boats were burned, thankfully, but Rick was beginning to earn (with this act and others) the hard-fought room to operate on the increasingly contentious flats.

"I tell young guys who ask me about guiding in Florida that they better be willing to play by the rules, but to never back down if the line gets crossed," says Rick.

"These new kids would make things a lot easier on themselves if they would just head down to Islamorada for their first season, pick out the toughest flats guide they can find, and beat the shit out of him. At

"I'm not sure, but how could you tell?"

"It's my job. A guide is supposed to know what's going on all around the boat, but the most important thing is what's happening on the bow. A good guide understands the body language of the angler standing up front, and never misses a thing. I want to know what the next cast is going to look like *before* it happens. I want to know if there'll be fire coming off that fly line."

Rick is right. Maybe it is the hot sun, maybe the fumes from the bug spray, but inevitably, you find yourself doing, thinking about, and saying things on the boat you wouldn't imagine doing or saying at the dinner table, or in the office. In this respect, the bow becomes the barber's chair or the psychiatrist's couch, a place to relieve the pressure of everyday life, but also a place to test personal and professional boundaries without the added expectations of formal manners or stilted etiquette. On the bow of Rick's skiff, for better or worse, you are encouraged to express yourself.

At times, having this personal daily theater unfold in front of him is the part of Rick's job he enjoys the most.

"Some days, you have to wonder what

some point, everyone has to stand their ground, and I'm not sure there's any reason in waiting 10 years to do it."

Why are your hands shaking?" Rick asks.

"Nervous."

"What for?"

would make a guy climb out of a warm bed and leave the wife and family behind at 4 a.m. You question the sanity of this," he explains. "I mean, flat's fishing is hard stuff, harder than most fishing. I'm not out hiding under the T-top like they do on the offshore boats.

"But this fishing is about freedom, and my office is 1.8 million acres big. I'm not the police; people are happy to be talking with me. And I get to see people at their best, when they're having fun, and also when they fail miserably and begin to question themselves. I see it all, but we learn, we get better, and we move on."

We spend an afternoon pressing further into the Keys in pursuit of some "bullet" bonefish, which means trading in the 11-weights for 8-weights, dabbing on new layers of sunblock, and ripping due south across Florida Bay where the water turns into an aquamarine tapestry of green channels, turquoise depressions, and tan, turtlegrass flats.

Rick poles downwind, looking for muds that indicate schools of bones feeding. We tie on a small brown shrimp pattern while our captain points out a flock of roseate spoonbills perched on a mangrove key, and explains that their bright pink plumage indicates an abundance of shrimp in the warm water shallows.

A half-dozen large bonefish are tailing ahead of us, their fins knifing through the wind-blown surface like cracked pieces of crystal. But they are spooky, and the light has turned against the wind, limiting our shots to opportunistic afterthoughts. It is hard to cut off Keys bonefish once they have made up their minds to avoid your position. "We'll stick tight and wait for another group," says Rick. "Chasing them with the boat is the ultimate act of desperation."

Finally, a lemon shark runs across the flat, promptly displacing our angling opportunities to deeper water. We have half a mind to get out the big rod and throw a fly at him but know without a steel leader, he only will chew it clean off. It isn't worth the effort or the cost of the fly this late in the day.

We decide to haul out ahead of the afternoon thundershowers and drive back to Homestead. Rick treats us to strawberry and banana-flavored milkshakes at a roadside fruit stand, and we pick up a few fresh man-

goes for breakfast. We make a toast to two productive days of fishing, writing, and photography. We have what we had come for, so we ask Rick what he wants to do in the morning.

He just smiles.

"I'll meet you at the gas station at 5 a.m."

Rick Murphy isn't satisfied yet. He says he'll be damned if his "tarpon shot" is going to be with a 60-pound fish. So we are back at the ramp in Flamingo before first light with a new plan. Rick says it is time to take the gloves off.

"You boys aren't opposed to a little baitfishing are you?" he asks, then supplies his own answer. "Good. 'Cause that's what we're going to do today."

Rick runs southwest from Flamingo toward the Oyster Keys, where he drops anchor, then throws out a small chum bag of frozen shrimp. He fashions two spinning rods with "sabiki" rigs (chains of jig-like hooks on fine leaders, some "freshened" with shrimp), then has us start cranking away for pinfish. The beautifully striped, palm-sized pinfish will be our tarpon bait. Rick says he prefers using sabiki rigs to

throwing the net—a net will knock the scales off the baitfish, and he wants the pinfish clean and full of energy.

It takes maybe 20 minutes before we have a couple dozen pinfish in the live well. Time to pack up and head north along the west side. We will cut through the mangroves and avoid the Gulf and waves.

But before the tarpon fishing starts, Rick idles the boat and pulls up alongside a mangled line of roots in the channel mouth. He sticks a poor pinfish on a steel hook and flips it toward the mangroves. Following the line on the water, we watch as the pinfish wriggles toward the presumed safety of the shoreline, but then abruptly puts on the brakes, spins around and starts wiggling back at the boat. Rick gives it another flip, then another, and each time, the same thing happens.

"It's just like I thought," smiles Rick. "There's a big snook hanging out in those roots. Pinfish doesn't want any part of him, and lucky for him, the snook isn't hungry, or he knows we're here."

Rick slips the hook out of the pinfish, and tosses him out into the channel, figuring he's had enough.

"Three tours of duty, and he's out. One more trip in there and that fish would've had a heart attack anyway."

Eventually, we find the bigger tarpon running down the Gulf's outside edge, between Middle Cape and East Cape. We stake out with our backs to the shoreline then begin throwing baseball-sized cork bobbers and hapless pinfish out into the Gulf with bait casting rods. We wait and watch as the bobbers drift on the tide, often tracking off in erratic directions, tethered five feet above the nervous bait. A tarpon rolls in close.

At once, the flat erupts like a geyser, sending the bobber flying 30 feet in one direction, the pinfish (or what's left of it) spiraling 30 feet in the opposite direction, and in the middle, the tarpon and the line shooting straight upward. It's a big one, over a hundred pounds, Rick shouts, as he cranks up the motor. We will have to run this fish down.

Jump, another jump, and another. "If you remember the jumps, you don't need anything else. It doesn't matter if you land them, but we're gonna land *this* fish."

The tarpon first runs deep, then makes a curious turn at the mangrove shoreline. "She's gonna try to wrap us up, break us off," mutters Murphy. When the tarpon wraps the line under a marled root, Murphy grabs the rod and threads it back through, never losing tension, and effectively trumping the fish's last ace.

That end game, when Captain Murphy grabs the leader, is when he is the most keyed up. "It's just you and me baby," he mutters. Then he clamps down with both hands on the tarpon's lower jaw and holds it in place. "When Rick Murphy grabs you with his hands, you know you've been grabbed," he smiles.

As the photographs are made, Rick quietly transitions from hunter to healer, gently rocking the fish back and forth in the water to get the water and oxygen flowing through her gills. Her large, black eyes are terrified and angry; most of her prehistoric scales have faded to a dingy gray. She is played out.

As we watch her slip away, we hope that she finds her strength before a bull shark or a hammerhead finds her. We all agree that we are played out as well.

Riding back toward Homestead, over the hammocks and through the Everglades pinelands, we pass a stand of dwarf cypress, which are telltales, not unlike the Spanish stopper trees, for the tarpon fishing. When dwarf cypress needles start to dry and brown, the tarpon season will begin to wane. It is a signal, says Rick, that winter's fragile grip on the Everglades and Keys will move the silver kings out to deeper water. He says it won't last long, and just as certain, the emergence of those first bright green needles on the dwarf cypress in late winter will signal the return of the kings to the shallows.

For Rick Murphy, the seasons, the islands, the flats, and the fish eventually blend together. He has to stop every now and again to look at the signs around him, if only to keep in tune with the ever changing cycles of life thriving on these flats, the Gulf, and throughout the enormous River of Grass.

We offer an invitation to our new friend.

"Hey Rick, you ought to come out and fish with us in Colorado someday."

He just smiles and says, "Thanks, but you know what I think about when I hear 'trout' don't you?"

"Bait."

"You got it. Bait. But I'm sure we'll be fishing together again before much longer... here."

He is right, as usual. Tarpon change lives.

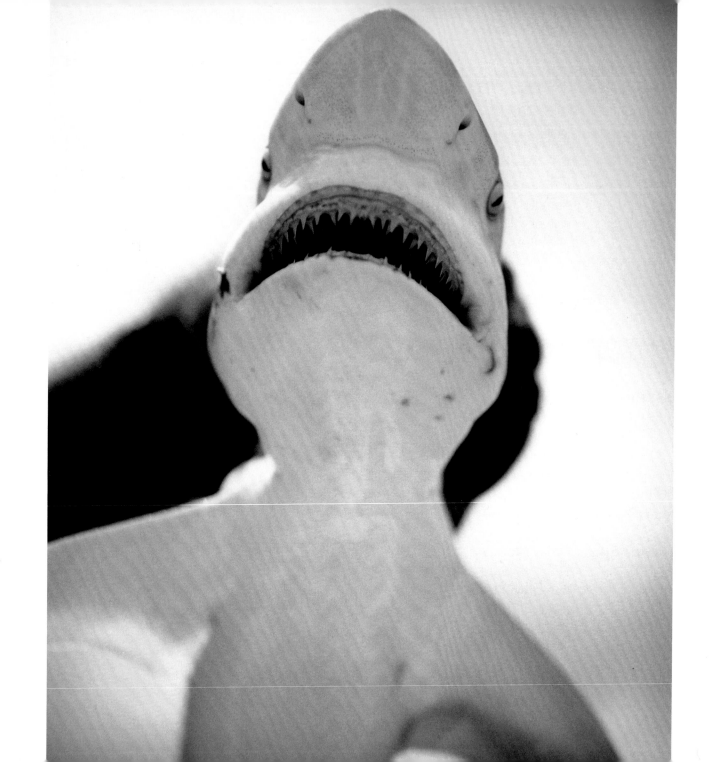

No Grand Slam Today

Wait out lightning squalls at dawn, bad cigarette smoke,

Flamingo boat ramp hostility, mosquitoes, borderline small talk

for the remote chance at a Florida Bay grand slam:

a bonefish, permit, and tarpon all leadered in one day.

By two o'clock, the mottled turquoise flats are a blast furnace,

leaving rays and only the sharks to eat, so we're headed in.

Understand what matters are the day's results, which are these:

zero permit, because they only exist in magazines or dreams;

two dozen fork-tailed bonefish spooked, lined, or bored;

thirteen tarpon jumped on baited pinfish, of those,

a fifty and eighty-pound fish landed, but babies hardly count;

a conventional rod stripped of guides then snapped against the boat;

ten sharks broken off, bulldozing toward the horizon.

These things would not be worth anyone's inventory:

seventy-five vultures tethered like black kites above Oyster Key;

the erratic way a pinfish swims when he's ready to be killed;

a burning limb of thunderhead arcing over Coastal Prairie like a warehouse fire;

twenty-five minutes reviving sea into a faded tarpon;

the sharks that will find her by electric smell or death's emissions;

the empty space of drifting sea she has left behind.

Gary Taylor
Slidell, Louisiana

Lake Borgne is choppy today, and it doesn't take much to get it roiled up. It is only several feet deep in most places, and a steady wind from almost any direction will turn the lake into a white-capped washboard with enough conflicting wave energy to cartwheel a bass boat nose over, or lift a deep-draft trawler onto a crest, then slam it down and crack its hull on the sandy bottom. Most days, it doesn't blow like this.

The computer had predicted a south wind. The television report said it would blow from the northwest. It is blowing southwest. Yet none of this matters to Gary Taylor. He already has figured out a place to fish, and more importantly, a way to get there. The *how you get there* is Gary Taylor's trademark.

One look at Gary's boat—or boats—moored in the marina, and you know you are not in for a typical day on the water. We climb aboard his Lafitte skiff, a Louisiana-born crabbing rig with a long, rounded hull and a wide profile that allows her to run in only two feet of water. Winched piggyback on the aft deck is a second (smaller) Hell's Bay flats fishing boat. The Lafitte skiff is Gary's workhorse ride across the voodoo chop of Lake Borgne; the Hell's Bay, his sleek and temperamental flats fishing machine.

The plan is simple: We will bust our way for an hour or more across the lake into the Bayou Biloxi Marsh, where the water flattens out into an almost infinite chain of rush and needlegrass islands, smooth sandy flats, and bug-infested channels. Once there, we will find a calm spot to anchor, slip the flats boat off the back, and start poling around to "see if we can't find us some reds."

We had heard from many people that Gary was an innovator extraordinaire, and witnessing his utilitarian approach unfold is proving the point. Waves begin slapping over the bow, throwing buckets of water against the wipers squeaking across the cockpit windshield. We ask Gary what we might find by way of numbers and size of redfish in the marsh, and how his fishing measures up against, say, Florida.

"We have so many more fish in Louisiana than Florida, it isn't even funny," he smiles. "If we had white sand beaches and snook, we'd shut Florida down."

Most fishing—certainly most saltwater fly-fishing—is the product of transposed ideas and techniques. For example, you can find yourself on a flat in Belize, in a skiff built in the Florida Keys, tying knots conceived decades ago by Venezuelan marlin fishermen, to connect leaders manufactured in Taiwan to fly patterns invented by a man in Pennsylvania, all in preparation for making a double-haul cast recently practiced on a river in Colorado, just as it was described by the California writer in a New York magazine article...

Gary Taylor's fishing, by contrast, is a more private, self-reliant enterprise, operating beyond the edge of industry endorsements. His organic approach is born of both necessity and experience, the result of a life spent on the unique bayous, marshes, lakes, and rivers of coastal Louisiana. He says knowing the subtle differences between Louisiana's waterways is the first step in learning to fish the area productively.

"A river, you know, is a big body of moving freshwater, a bayou is a smaller creek or tributary, a marsh is a plain of water with grassy islands but no trees, and a swamp is a flooded forest," he explains. "There's a special boat for every piece of water, and we'll find different fish in all of 'em."

The Taylors have lived in Slidell, east of New Orleans, for four generations, and Gary is the third generation to live on his property. He learned to fish these home waters not long after he learned to ride a bike. Every summer, his father would pack up the family the day after school let out, and they would head off to "camp" on an island for several weeks.

Gary Taylor

It was in these early days when Gary learned to pole a boat, not a flats boat, but a "pirot," a flat bottom dugout specifically designed to maneuver through the confined waterways of Louisiana's backcountry. He explains how his buddy and he used to drop their pirots in the water two days apart from each other, and hunt and fish their ways to a meeting point somewhere in the middle. Back in those days, Gary caught so many redfish, he considered them garbage fish.

"My mother made coubion [fish stew] so often, I started breakin' off reds on purpose so I wouldn't have to eat 'em anymore."

The Louisiana water (and its fishing) put a permanent lock on Gary Taylor. Years back, he joined the professional bass fishing tour, then, 14 years ago, entered the world of guiding for money. Still, he contends that his interest in fishing is less a professional pursuit than an addiction to the thrill of the chase, a connection with his culture, and a deep-seeded fascination with things that swim.

As he tells us how he once made an artificial bass pond by filling his backyard pool with Christmas trees, we have difficulty removing from our minds the image of Richard Dreyfus in *Close Encounters of the Third Kind* frenetically constructing a Devil's Tower replica in his living room with heaping piles of mud and shrubbery.

"Once it's in you, you can't shake it," Gary smiles. "You realize that you're thinking about the water and the fish so much, you might as well go for it and make it a business."

Which is why Gary named his business "Go For It Charters." The fly-fishing wrinkle has evolved from conventional approaches over time, at first sporadically, then consistently, as he developed a dedicated and forgiving clientele willing to learn and grow into this hi-tech sport along with him. In subsequent years, he has used this on-the-job training to develop boxes of deadly, no-name fly patterns, reliable fishing techniques, and a fleet of fish chasing kayaks, pontoons, catamarans, and skiffs, all adapted to pursue Biloxi Marsh redfish in any conceivable condition.

Not surprisingly, Gary shrugs off the suggestion that his improvisations put him ahead of the mainstream.

"I know I've spent a whole lot of time devisin' different ways to get after these reds, but one thing's for sure, I've never been boat-poor, and I am thankful for that."

A 360-degree scan of the horizon reveals only one other boat in this part of the marsh, a small crabber, way off on the eastern horizon. Our only other visible company, a white ibis, mechanically pokes along a spartina grass shoreline.

"What we might oughta do is go 'round on the other side of this island and get out of the wind some. I'm willin' to bet my bottom dollar that the water will be cleaner over there in about an hour or so," Gary suggests.

And with that, he fires up the little engine and races us through a labyrinth of narrow channels, throwing the Hell's Bay up on port edge to peel around one bank, then on starboard edge to avoid the next. In a matter of minutes, he slows the skiff to enter a hidden, twenty-acre bay. At the moment, the water is not much cleaner, but the tide is still up. No dorsal fins, tails, or other visible signs of redfish, but Gary is certain they are here.

We make a few blind casts against the bank, and every once in a while, the effort is rewarded with a redfish that eats an orange tinsel fly. It is proof, says Gary, that the old saying is true—even a blind pig finds an acorn every now and again. We decide to stay put and wait a while.

Just as he predicted, it takes nearly an hour for the tide to drop, and when it does, the water is still not transparent enough to reveal the silhouettes of redfish. Gary directs our eyes and attention toward the shoreline, submerged oyster beds, and creek mouths. Slowly, we begin to see subtle wakes, copper flashes, and every so often, tails—dozens of them, right in front of us. The fish had been here all along.

In the far reaches of the bay, over a sandbar and out of reach for us to pole in this falling tide, we see a lone redfish. He is so big, more than half his black-backed body is exposed from the water. He oozes his way over mud and up into the weeds, almost amphibian in his approach, lazily feeding on shrimp and blue crabs that pour through the retreating currents. Gary calls these fish "crawlers."

"What does that mean?"

"It means if I was in my kayak right now, it'd be his ass."

Redfish, also called red drum, are much like backcountry Louisiana in their resilience and subtle, primal beauty. At first glance, they are not a particularly noble-looking fish, some even say they aren't far from being carp-ugly. But close examination reveals how their oversized, almost prehistoric scales display a muted array of earthy tones, a complex mosaic of pinks, browns, yellows and tans, ultimately accentuated by the trademark "false eye" black spots on their tails, created with the evolutionary purpose of confusing predators into striking away from the fish's vulnerable brain and eyes.

Though not the toughest fighters in the ocean, and without a thoroughbred's endurance, the redfish is a rugged survivor. They can adapt to rapid environmental changes that would pressure most other fish to migrate, or die off altogether. A red can survive in water less than 50 degrees Fahrenheit as easily as it can in water approaching 90 degrees. With compact, muscular, buoyant and balanced bodies,

they have an uncanny ability to hoist themselves over the shallowest flats, even burrow into mangroves or grassy shorelines to root out shrimp and crabs most other fish would not threaten.

Louisiana redfish are not discriminating eaters, allowing for generous, year-round growth and excellent "catching" opportunities for the angler. They can smell, see, and feel (through vibrations) food, which they snatch off the bottom with their undershot, vacuum-like mouths, then pulverize with rows of crushers placed at the backs of their throats. If you land a fly near a redfish, somewhere they can feel it, they very often will turn and chase as if someone just rang the dinner bell and, depending on the angler's point of view, this come-and-get-it nature of the redfish is either their greatest attribute or weakness.

Gary Taylor considers the "forgiving" nature of the redfish to be a blessing.

"I understand why people want to fish for permit, bonefish, and such," he explains. "You need to capture that elusive fish, but elusive is frustrating, and for me, catching fish is fun too. I think more fun that way."

"After all, they call 'Nawlins "The Big Easy," don't they?"

Truth be told, we had made our pilgrimage to New Orleans the previous evening, if only to satisfy a little train-wreck fascination with the Bacchanalian arts, pick up some Mardi Gras beads, and maybe a little positive French Quarter ju-ju, which never hurts on a fishing boat. Eventually, we returned to Slidell early, near models of temperance, realizing after all that we were "on the job."

Despite its proximity, Gary does not often venture into the Crescent City, not like he did back in his "Comanche Indian days."

"At some point, I realized that you'll come closer to catchin' all the redfish in the marsh than drinkin' all the liquor on Bourbon Street," he laughs.

So now we have turned our attention to a pair of redfish working along the bank. Gary says it is a perfect setup. Schools of redish are tricky, because you have to pick the lead fish and make an accurate shot; singles are wary and spook easily, but doubles are aggressive and will compete for food. We make one cast and the bank-side fish darts

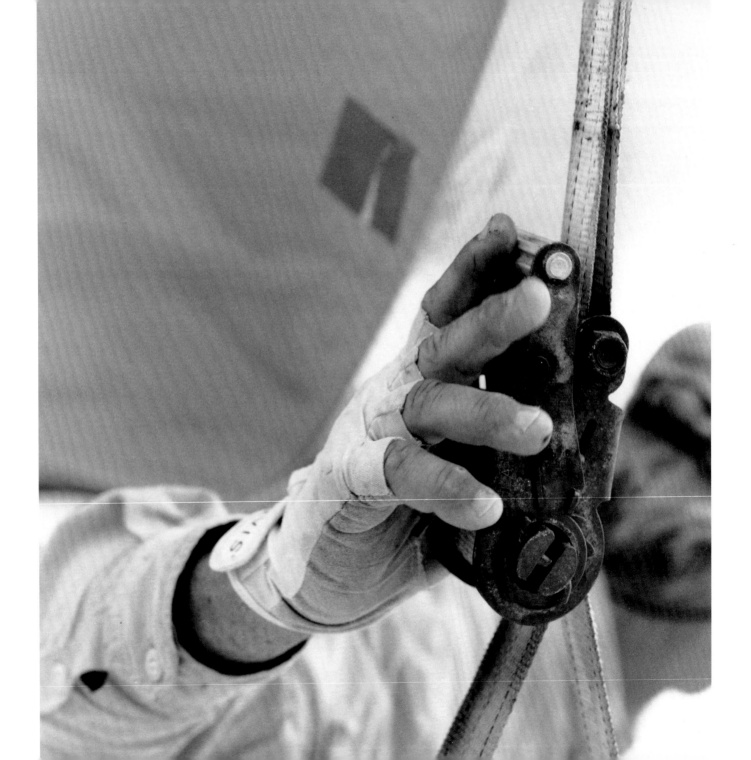

over and steals the fly in a split second. Realizing he's hooked, the generous (30-inch, 12-pound) red boils over in a series of uneven tumbles and thrashes, peeling the line in a taught arc back along the bank, and sending the startled other fish on a nervous bee-line to God-knows-where.

"What do I do? You want this rod low or high? Do you want him on the reel? Should I try to steer him to the middle?" the angler shouts over his shoulder, hungry for instruction.

"Just crank him in, and let's not worry about it," Gary whispers. "I'll let you know when we get a *real* fish on. This one's just a baby."

When Gary Taylor says a big red is "30," he means pounds, not inches, but he is quick to point out that Louisiana redfish come in all sizes. The "rat reds" are the little ones, maybe two or three pounds, while an average fish from the marsh runs about six pounds. The big bulls, or "crawlers," start at 10 pounds and run well over 40. He has caught them as large as "48" on the fly, but those fish are not to be expected often, if ever.

Of course, seeing and catching fish that large are two entirely different propositions. Gary tells us that when the big tails come wallowing down the bank, poking up and waving like bright blue paddle blades, even the best anglers are susceptible to the flats fishing equivalent of "buck fever."

Some fishermen are able to make the difficult, one-time cast, while others are not. The odd thing, says Gary, is that some of the people who are able to make the cast do so because they have no idea what they're doing, completely unaware of the pressure-filled expectations of the situation. Many others, however, (often, excellent anglers) become so consumed with impressing the guide, their partners, or themselves, that they seize up at the moment of truth.

"I'd rather see you blow the deal at least tryin' than to completely tense up when it's time to cast," admits Gary. "I remember one time I had these guys who could really cast, but whenever we'd see a decent red, they couldn't even get the fly out of the boat.

"I ended up backin' up the skiff and takin' a time out. I said, 'Boys, we need to take a break here. It's supposed to be fun. It's *only* redfish.'"

"The bottom line is that you don't need some guy back up on the push pole chewin' your ass out whenever we see a decent fish. These reds, especially the crawlers, will make people nervous enough."

Later, we watch a pair of bottle-nosed dolphins patrol the entrance to a bay, no doubt waiting to ambush a wayward redfish or two, and it begs the question: "Hey Gary, what eats the redfish in this marsh?"

"Mostly just porpoises and Cajuns," he laughs.

In truth, humans have been—and remain—the most serious threat to redfish in Louisiana. Perhaps the fish's fatal flaw is the fact that it tastes so good. When the "blackened redfish" culinary craze took off decades ago, the commercial and recreational pressure nearly decimated the species. It only has been within the past decade, with the implementation of tougher commercial regulations, that the reds have made a dramatic rebound, highlighting again the resiliency of the species.

Gary concedes that the system still hangs by a thread, particularly in parts of the country where people accept and expect things to be managed the way they have been, for years and years. In practice, some rules and regulations are arbitrarily enforced with a wink and smile. Like the story of Slidell Captain X, who is hauled in on Monday for using illegal seine nets, brought before the judge (his brother-in-law) on Wednesday, and picks up his confiscated nets behind the courthouse later that afternoon. It happens all the time, says Gary.

Which, ultimately, is why he chooses to run way out here to the marsh, to fish in waters most recreational fishermen won't bother reaching, and most commercial boats won't risk running aground in. You can be frustrated, or you can work around reality, says Gary. But there will be a day of reckoning, particularly if the commercial captains have their way and the already liberal redfish catch limits are relaxed even further, as proposed.

"I understand that Louisiana embraces a meat fishing mentality, but there comes a point when you have to look further down

the road than tomorrow or next season. Otherwise we'll all wake up with no fish, and that's when everybody will be looking for answers."

"You can't manage a redfish fishery out of nothin', or ever hope to bring it back when zero equals zero equals zero… That's the simplest equation in the world."

It isn't easy to fight conventional thinking. Gary tells us the story about fishing for spotted seatrout with a regular client, a well-heeled businessman from New Orleans, who hooked and landed his eighteenth fish, and immediately went searching for the ice-chest.

"Hell, why don't you just do everyone a favor and throw him up on the bank and let the coons have at him," Gary said.

"What?"

"You heard what I said. You'll take that fish home and put him in your freezer, where it'll get freezer burn, and you'll just end up throwin' it away in three months, just like you throw away all the others, when it's time to come back down here and go fishing again."

For Gary, confidence, not dead fish, is the ultimate measure of a fishing captain's or fisherman's skill. Acquiring this confidence, however, is a process that happens over years, not weeks, and is likely to entail growing pains, says Gary. A few years back, some of the local commercial captains sitting at the Slidell marina, drunk on Dixie Beer, began heckling Gary about another day on the water catching and releasing redfish.

"Where's all them reds you caught today?" the captains laughed.

"Let 'em all go."

"You ain't catchin' no fish…"

"Well, I'll tell you what. I got a hundred bucks here that says if we head back out on the water right now, I can put more fish in the cooler than anyone in this marina."

"Hundred bucks ain't worth crankin' up the boat," one shouted. "'Specially when you got nothin' to prove how good you are."

"Well, I guess we better head right over to the bank then, so we can crank this mother up for a thousand?"

Stunned silence.

"I haven't had any more problems from that bunch since."

Gary Taylor

By the last day, we had battled enough big fish that we never again would doubt the stories of monster reds being caught in Louisiana on the fly. We leave the rods at the hotel and let Gary make the call on where to go. He chooses the swamp.

He trailers a flat-bottom johnboat to a nondescript bridge pull-off on the "east-middle" branch of the Pearl River, and from here, we slowly motor up the main channel until the river narrows into a maze of amber water, walled in on all sides by tupelo and black gums, cypress trees, and thickets of brush. Spider lilies blossom in sporadic white bursts among the black, brown, and dark green shadows.

We see deer drinking from the swamp, terrapins crawling up banks, alligators sliding under deadfall, and snakes—diamondback water snakes and water moccasins—sunning themselves in loose, nondescript coils, massed on stumps at water's edge. None of us can remember an experience when we had chanced upon poisonous snakes in the wild, but had not been afraid or startled.

Maybe it is the place, or maybe it is the way we move, but for the first time in our lives, we agree the snakes are strangely beautiful.

We begin to realize Gary's motive. It isn't so much that he wants to initiate us to the swamp's staggering tapestry of life (that much was obvious) as much as he hoped to reveal momentary windows—like ancient family photographs—into the raw timeless-ness of Louisiana's backcountry, and more privately, into the dark, tannic waters where he learned to fish, hunt, and pole pirots as a child. Like any individual proud of their ancestry, Gary wants us to see the home water he had grown up on, water, he says, that really hasn't changed a whole lot since the Colapissas once lived here.

It seems that, if the story is about the man, it starts with knowing the land and the water, and it is here where you have the best chance to glimpse upon an individual's soul. Gary may hope that we are able to see something beyond the fishing, the boats and lines, the coolers full of fish— and our hope now is that he understands we do.

Crawler

Most of the year the marsh is full of pretty decent reds,

but what we look for—out near the Gulf—are the big bulls

or crawlers half in the cordgrass workin' their way

down a shoreline eatin' blue crabs, shrimp, mullet,

or just about anything they can get their crushers on.

With that big back and blue tail stickin' up through the grass,

you can't hardly miss a good crawler unless you're blind or asleep,

and even then, he'll eat your Chicken if you give him half a chance.

A lot of times, especially these trout fisherman, have to know

which way a crawler is headed or what he's fixin' to eat,

and what you need to do is just get that damn fly

in the water and stop makin' all that commotion on the boat,

because these big ones hear almost anything, and they know better.

Last week we had the wind lay down for a day or two,

and there were a mess of bugs for sure, but we took

a seventeen, a nineteen, a twenty, a twenty-two, and a thirty

when the water was right, and that's a good pile of crawlers.

Those are times the big bulls move thirty, sometimes

forty feet to come get a fly because they're really on the feed.

That's when you look at a crawler and say dead meat,

that's when you know you fished redfish in Louisiana.

Jeff Heyer
Nantucket, Massachusetts

The scant outline of Nantucket materializes through a heavy, morning fog, and we are able to make out the grassy, windswept bluffs, weathered lighthouses, and breakwaters at the harbor mouth. We feel relieved. Leaning over the rails of the ferry, we find ourselves imagining what it must have felt like 150 or more years ago, to return from a whaling voyage that had lasted years and likely claimed lives, to finally behold the welcoming silhouette of this island. Among the first manmade structures that come into view are the church steeples, which seem profoundly appropriate, even for us.

Nantucket will be a waypoint, a four-day layover on our journey. And while the travails we encountered to get here were relative child's play, we are no less grateful to reach the dock.

We are a day late thanks to a Sunday storm (nobody called it a nor'easter until the ferry boat was loaded, then ordered to stay in Hyannisport) that had left us stuck on Cape Cod. Word was that the ferry captain was ready to make the run, even though the wind was gusting over 50 miles an hour. Crew members rolled their eyes as they chained the cars to the lower deck. The passengers who realized what this tempest would do to the ocean (create a volatile, perhaps dangerous, and certainly uncomfortable heap of waves in the shallow straight) had found all the good seats, the ones closest to the head or near the rail. Evidently the Coast Guard called us off, and we all spun around and climbed back off the boat. The three of us found a room and went looking for Quahog chowder.

Jeff Heyer did not expect us. He could

tell by the wind on his kitchen window that the ocean had become nearly impassable.

"You guys didn't want to come over in that mess anyway," he says, when we finally meet up. "We can make up for lost time, and we'll still find fish. There's plenty to go around in Nantucket."

We are not sure whether he means plenty of lost time or plenty of fish. Probably both, we reckon.

Jeff Heyer steps out from behind the counter at Cross Rip Outfitters, his well-dressed fly shop on a cobbled corner in Nantucket town. At once he impresses us with a soft-spoken, low-key and pragmatic demeanor. He also exudes an unmistakable directness and honesty; he says he has to check with the "boss" about when to be back. His wife, Lynne, says we can keep him all day.

Jeff runs us through a brief personal and fishing history as we wind along narrow, overgrown roads among the standard gray shake-shingled houses, past cranberry bogs and meadows, and finally into the boat yard at Madaket Harbor.

He grew up in New Jersey. His family has enjoyed fishing and the outdoors for many years, especially offshore fishing, and it was several years ago, while competing here in a bluewater tournament, when he met Lynne. Lynne is a native islander, and was raised (like most Nantucket children) with a strong sense of the island's fishing and whaling history and traditions. As a little girl, Lynn learned to scrimshaw decorative ivory for the tops of light ship baskets, to hunt shorelines for clams and mussels, and to spot swordfish amongst the ocean swells from the crow's nests of offshore boats. She's always been the best at spotting fish, Jeff says.

Together, they opened the store several years ago, and now maintain a life of seasons, beginning the year in spring, running full speed through the busy summer months, slowing (a little) to squeeze in some duck hunting in the fall, and then packing up for the Florida Keys after the holidays. We ask Jeff if he ever gets island fever.

"I'm on the boat as much as I'm on the island," he answers with a smile. "To be honest, when the season is going strong, I'm too busy to worry about it, and when it slows down, we go to Florida and hunt tarpon. I wish I had more time to sleep, but I just haven't found any yet."

It still will be a few weeks before the most important Nantucket season—the tourist season—begins in earnest. By the Fourth of July, the island's population will swell to over 50,000 people, and the Heyers will be running on all cylinders. Jeff says he often will run three "half-day" trips in a single day, starting on the water at 4:30 a.m. and not quitting until after 9 p.m. It is then he says he gets irritable and a bit burned out, but on this day in early June, watching him smile as he steers the boat through a mid-morning haze, it is hard to imagine that is possible.

The seasons of Nantucket are fairly predictable. As for striped bass, Jeff says the schoolies usually arrive by late April; the bigger cruisers roll in a few weeks later. By the third week of May, the bluefish appear, again the smaller ones show up first. The human wave arrives around Memorial Day (they come in all sizes), though the heavy run won't start until the third week in June, once schools let out. By the third week in July, the Atlantic bonita arrive. The bluefin tuna swim in by July-August. Little tunny, the false albacore, roll through in early September, and, in doing so, displace the less

aggressive bonita. By October, fish and people are usually headed off to other places.

Jeff says these days in late spring are for scouting. The storms and the constant parade of powerful flood and ebb tides scrubbing back and forth along the island change this seascape in real time. The sand bar that was here last year may now be 500 yards away, or washed out altogether. The sandy bottom of Nantucket's perimeter is constantly changing. In the early days, the volatile and shifting nature of these waters led to their notoriety as some of the most difficult to navigate in the northeast. Today, it is a simpler challenge for the charter captain.

"Every year, I have to re-learn the water," explains Jeff. "Part of living in Nantucket is learning to survive and adapt to the constantly changing ocean, but imagine what navigating these waters was like a hundred and fifty years ago with wooden boats and without technology. We have it pretty easy."

It only takes a few minutes to reach the other side of Madaket harbor. Jeff wants to fish along the west edge, in the lea, figuring the schoolies might run the beach on this falling tide. In the worst case, he knows they'll hold over in deep water. We will throw sinking-tipped fly lines and large Sea Habbits, and, hopefully, sight a few stripers cruising the barren shorelines and drop-offs.

But the light isn't perfect, and the wind and rain are making things downright bitter. It is cold and damp, with not enough rain to rinse the salt taste off your lips, but enough cool moisture in the air that you can see every breath. You can't have it all your way, Jeff says, and in Nantucket, there usually is something—wind, or rain, or the tide—working against the angler. It is a mistake to hope for everything to line up just right. Here, you persevere.

"The perfect day is when you have full sun, no clouds, lots of moving water, five-to ten-knot winds, and pleasant temperatures. You can try as hard as you want to anticipate days like that, but I've learned that's nearly impossible. You just have to recognize and enjoy good luck when it happens," says Jeff.

We ask Jeff how many perfect days he gets in a season. He thinks three, maybe four.

"And you still like fishing out here?"

"Sure, because when things aren't

perfect, you're learning. On a perfect day you're simply enjoying. I'd rather spend 50 days turning up new challenges on these waters when things *aren't* perfect. It makes me a better captain, and when you fish Nantucket, you better be ready for a few surprises."

The rain takes a short breather, and the clouds begin to break up, filtering a dozen columns of light over the bay. We see striper shadows under the surface. Jeff calls the first shot: It is a decent bass, 50 feet away at 10 o'clock from the bow.

The angler pulls the sluggish line off the deck and starts rolling casts back and forth until there is enough line played out to tighten the loop and zero in on target. The three-inch, blue fly lands in the neighborhood, but the shadow detours, and motors off to deep water.

"Lined him," Jeff whispers.

"Damn."

"There's another at 11 o'clock, a bit closer. Pick it up and try him."

This cast falls just inside the next fish, which methodically looks upward at the splash, follows the fly as it cascades down-

ward for a second or two, then takes it with a lunge, flaring his gills, mouth gaping for a split second, then snapping shut around the fly. The slack fly line burns fingers as it rips through the guides and out the end of the rod. Still going. Still going.

"Think he'll stop?"

"When you make him," laughs Jeff. The battle lasts several minutes, long enough to indoctrinate us to the uniquely subtle appeals of this game, and instill a sense of genuine respect for the striper. This isn't the biggest fish, but a decent one, maybe 32 inches, and 12 pounds. From our angle, with the striper's body folded underneath his broad, muted green head, he looks like an olive floating at the bottom of a dirty martini.

"You'll be playing that take over and over when you turn in tonight," Jeff says, as he releases the fish. "It'll be sweet dreams when you see that fish again."

The striped bass is not the biggest, nor the fastest ocean fish you will catch, but he is plenty strong for his size. He has a thick, muscular body, like a linebacker, and an uncanny ability to cut, weave, and, most importantly, react to almost any given situa-

tion. He thrives in a variety of coastal environments. Born in the estuary, the striper likes to cruise the bays and shallows in search of sand eels and anchovies, but he also thrives in tidal rips, drop-offs, and deep water, where he is just as willing to ambush squid and menhaden.

Each spring and summer, the striper ranges hundreds of migratory miles in search of food. On the Atlantic Coast, they span from the St. Lawrence Seaway to northern Florida. The Chesapeake Bay was the original home of the species, once accounting for roughly 90 percent of the striped bass spawning and reproduction in the east.

Near Nantucket, you will find him right off the beach, or out in the rips and cross-currents, holding steady with a broad, muscular tail in water so turbid it disorients other species, rendering them helpless to avoid the striper's attack.

Morone saxtalis (striper, rockfish, linesider, roller, squidhound, and greenhead) is, perhaps, one of the most easily recognized saltwater fish. With several trademark black lateral lines raked like planted rows along each flank, his body is accentuated by a spiney dorsal fin, vibrant shades of silver along its sides, a bright white belly, and a greenish hue across his blocky forehead. He is not timid by any stretch, but he's no fool, and he'll challenge any angler to make accurate casts in tough places. When you hook your first decent striper, he likely will be in charge for the first few moments, instantaneously instilling a sense of respect that dogs many anglers throughout their lives.

"There aren't many fish that could survive the changes in temperature, weather, and ocean we have here on the east coast, and specifically Nantucket," Jeff says. "But the striper has found a way to do it, and you must respect him for that accomplishment. Pound for pound, I don't think you'll find a tougher fish in the ocean."

Walking along the eastern shore of the island, between Siasconset and Quidnet, we watch rare piping plovers and least terns flush along the sand and through the grasses, and then fly in sweeping circles overhead. Nantucket and its waters provide sanctuary to many threatened creatures, and ironically, whales are now among them.

Far off on the horizon, we spot the spouts from a pod of whales. We had been told that you can tell the type of whales by the patterns of spray from their blowholes. A sperm whale, for example, blows at an angle. Others will exhale water and air like geysers, shooting straight upward in a pillar, while others will create a fountain, or umbrella pattern. Thus, the old whalers could tell what they were chasing from a distance, before they lowered the harpoon boats over the sides of the main ship. These whales are breaching. Our best guess is that they are humpbacks. They never come close enough for us to determine for sure, though we watch for a half hour or more.

Jeff Heyer has seen and heard the whales, many times close enough to touch them. He describes for us how, further offshore, you can chance upon whales, and if you look close enough, see big bluefish and stripers drafting behind the pods, pouncing on baitfish that have moved in to gorge on displaced krill. It is common to see big stripers, fifty pounds or better, among the whales. It is also dangerous and against the law to fish for them, though some people undoubtedly take their chances.

It is when you see the whales up close, says Jeff, that so much about Nantucket, the sea, and the cycles of life that revolve around this island come into clearest focus. He recounts for us the experience how, a few summers ago, a pod of blackfish (pilot whales) had beached themselves on Nantucket. He was among the dozens of volunteers who tried to save the creatures in vain. As the experts traded theories and explanations, ultimately arguing over what to do, Jeff was among the locals who stayed up all night, listening to the dying animals as they slowly suffocated in the darkness, figuring that a bullet in every blowhole probably was the most humane answer. The next morning, he wrestled to hold their enormous tails still, as they were given lethal injections.

"I'll never forget that experience, and the sounds and smell on that beach," says Jeff. "The whales are smart animals, and very mysterious. They have this ability to make you aware that humans are only one part of a very large, and not so understood picture."

We spend an afternoon fishing outside the shelter of the harbors and bays, out toward Tuckernuck, among the rips and

shoals, where a mixture of ruddy to blonde harbor, harp, gray, and hooded seals play along sandy islands that stretch toward Martha's Vineyard.

The ocean raises its voice here, especially during the flood tide, arguing with the wind, loud enough to drown out the whirs of the engine, as Jeff slips his boat in and out of gear, running to the crests of swells, then retreating with the foamy water as it pours off the sands. The goal is to cast when the boat rides the crest, and strip the fly back with the receding water. But the motion of the boat mixing and bumping in the conflicting currents is awkward and violent, making the act of fly casting akin to riding a bull and playing a violin simultaneously.

Jeff shouts: "Here comes a good one, hang on, and when it picks us up, shoot that fly as far as you can, up there in the foam, and start stripping it back. Okay, ready …" We feel the boat lifting, as if it were being raised by a forklift, then hear the engine clunk into gear. Still rising, engine starting to growl, the wave begins to break. "Now!"

And in that one hot second, when all the water surges underneath us, we hustle a cast on the point. The floor drops, and the wave pours over the shoal, first obscuring it within the gray wall, then washing through, leaving a scoured sheen of mottled foam thigh-deep over the bar.

The fly lands where we hoped it would, and somehow, within four strips, it is found and swallowed by a bass that had been feeding methodically within the chaos. She runs hard off the shoal, against the current, showing us a good measure of backing, before turning back on the rip. The move allows us to gather some line, but only momentarily, before she makes a second run, then a third. Jeff lands and admires three feet of lean, sculpted striper, before a group of seals pull in and run the remaining life off the shoal.

The next morning, Jeff drifts us along the northern edge of the island, up toward Great Point, in search of bluefish. The sea birds hovering nearby indicate blues in this water, but there isn't a telltale slick, nervous water, or anything else that visibly would catch our attention. So we ride the tide, throwing a de-hooked jig with a spinning rod, hoping to tease a stray bluefish close enough to the boat so that we might hit him with a fly. It works.

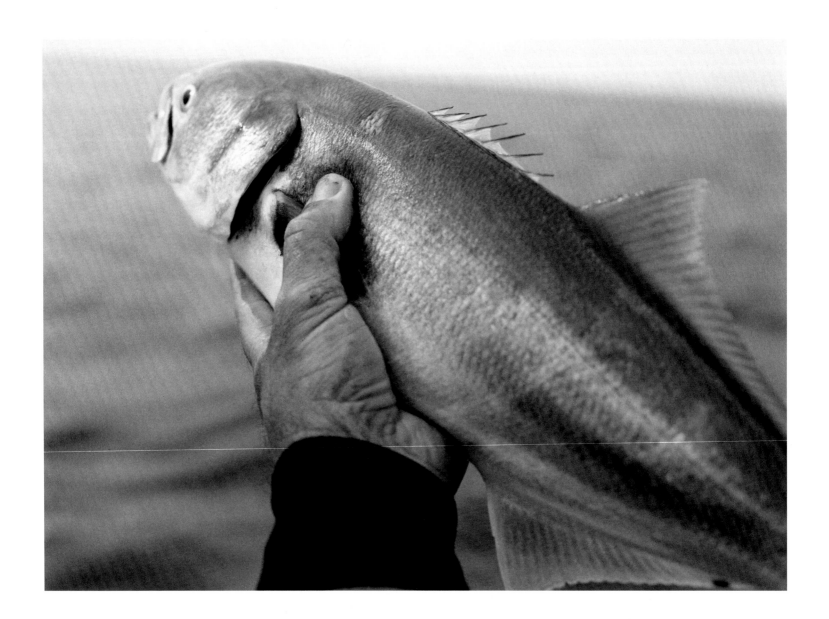

The bluefish we catch are scout-sized, forerunners to the bigger fish that will pour off these banks in another month or two. But they fight hard. Bluefish always do.

"Bluefish are some of the most underrated fish in the ocean," says Jeff as he unhooks one, careful to keep a firm grip behind its gills, and using pliers to remove the hook from its rows of tiny, saw blade teeth. "These guys get a bad rap, but pound-for-pound they pull pretty hard and always eat with abandon. Anyone can catch a bluefish, even kids, and it's hard not to like that."

We notice another boat, idling in our direction. We still haven't figured out how this saltwater game is played. It is, at times, disconcerting how the boats will circle around each other, like hyenas loitering on the edge of the lion pride, waiting for something to happen. And when the action starts, many have no qualms about moving in on the others. Jeff takes it in stride.

He says trout fishermen like us have to understand that when the bite is on, it is a temporary, mobile phenomenon. You have to take advantage when you can. It isn't like the river, where you can yield a run, know-

ing you can return a few hours later, and the fish will be stacked in there, just like they were yesterday, just like they will be tomorrow.

Besides, there are ways to throw off the competition. For example, you can crush up a bag of potato chips and throw it overboard. He says Lay's work best.

"They create an oily slick in the water and attract flocks of diving birds, just like a

school of bluefish crashing menhaden," Jeff laughs. "You would be surprised how often this ruse saves the day during the crowded summer months."

On the last evening, Jeff weaves his boat through the harbor, drops us off at a no-name dock at the edge of town, and tells us how to find the car. He says he'll meet us at 7 o'clock, which gives us enough time to ride back to Siasconset, change into dry clothes and return to town.

We share stories with Jeff and Lynne at the Lobster Pot, talking about what most fishermen talk about—far away places, seen and unseen, and big fish, real or imagined. That night, the stripers do return in our dreams, just like Jeff said they would, swimming between the conscious reality and unconscious imagination, where they belong.

Uncle Peter drives us to the dock in the morning, and we catch the early ferry, the fast boat, for the mainland. When the engines kick to life as we round through the harbor inlet, it doesn't take long for the shoreline to begin fading back into oblivion, into that fog-shrouded outline that we had contemplated upon our arrival. Only now the feeling is completely different. There is no relief, but also no strong sense of sadness. Only wonder. We wonder if we'll ever come back. We think we will.

We know Nantucket will change. Maybe not in terms of its facades and landscapes; what's seen above the ocean's surface will, no doubt, be painstakingly preserved for many generations to come. But the waters will evolve, shift, and contort the hidden character of this place.

We, frankly, had been surprised by the richness of this ocean texture, the quality of the fishing, and perhaps, even by the deftness and understated character of our friend and guide. If ever there were a place worth rediscovering on a regular basis, and a person worth doing that with, they are Nantucket, and Jeff Heyer.

To Know a Nantucket Striper

When the tide falls off a shoal near the north
arm of Tuckernuck Island—heavy like prairie thunder,
streaming hysterical bait, the glacier blue current
cut in half and half again by the accordioned,
lice-covered tails of stripers—you will find
fish in the rusted iron crease of a sea angel's wing.

Bleed out a striper's black, all-American blood
through a dirty engine well drain plug into the sea.
Watch the golden, feral ring of her iris fade miserably grey.
Strip her spine and leather skin of expensive dinner flanks.
Remember her light green head knocking underneath the boat.

We would catalog Thoreau's landscape—treeless plains
of lonesome poverty-grass; an abandoned, weather-stained
house standing against wind and sea; the metallic calls
of mackerel-gulls; the vertebrae, sinews, and iron jaw
of a Nauset woman; breakers looking like a thousand
wild horse manes; bluefish butchery and menhaden
oil slicks; one hundred and eighty blackfish run ashore;
the ocean's heaped up rut; a rib of bleached whale bone
woven through a road-side fence—but there is a job to do:
find a school of stripers and make them eat.

Al Keller
Naples, Florida

The alligators look like old, faded tractor tires stuck in the mud and canal water, as we drive the Tamiami Trail through tribal swamplands and toward Everglades City and Chokoloskee Island. Passing the Rod & Gun Club, then rows of stilted houses, we stop at the historic Smallwood Store, the site where the Chokoloskee locals killed Mr. Watson almost a century ago.

A few dollars will get you a walk through this diorama of Florida settler life, preserved like a stuffed fish hanging on the wall. It gives you a sense of what used to be, when this part of the country was home to plot farmers, moonshiners, bird hunters, and fugitives, people tough enough (or desperate enough) to live in ragged harmony with the Everglades, three-steps removed from mainland society.

Back then, this place offered haven, and it still does to some degree, though in a different way. If you really want to see and feel this area's history, living not preserved, you must head out, through the channels and bays, into the 10,000 Islands. It is here, among the storks and alligators, in the red mangroves, and on the flat, tea-colored water, where you have the best shot at finding true solitude, or an unfiltered window into the Everglades storied past.

As we drive north toward Goodland, past airboat billboards, convenience store gas stations, and miles and miles of empty swamp and overgrown marshes, we feel a sense of homecoming because most of what little saltwater fishing we had experienced in years past had been in the 10,000 Islands, and most of that from the deck of Al Keller's boat.

The cell phone rings; it's Al.

"Meet me at the marina at 7 o'clock,"

he says. "We have a falling tide in the morning, and I'm pretty sure you won't have any trouble finding me. I might be the only boat there."

Do not let the clean-cut look or boyish laugh fool you—Al Keller is an authentic Florida flats guide. He was born in Miami, raised in Tampa, and has fished most of the saltwater flats and back bays between the two cities. He learned young, back in the days when he and his friends used to have day-long competitions to see who could walk around small mangrove islands by balancing only on the roots; if you touched the water, you lost.

Today, Al is still a betting man. He laughs as he recounts the story from last spring, after the tarpon showed up on the flats, how he and another captain laid 20-dollar bills on the table, and said the first man to land a tarpon with a client would collect. Twenty minutes after they left the marina, Al was on the radio.

"I said 'game over," laughs Al. "I had seen these tarpon a few days before, and waited until I had a trip with this guy who I knew was a good fisherman before I made

the bet. It wasn't a big fish, but we hooked him on the first cast."

Perhaps his biggest gamble is his willingness to adhere to fly-fishing in a world where it makes better business sense for a captain to employ more conventional approaches. Most of the clients who charter trips from Goodland want to catch fish, pure and simple, and even those who call themselves fly-fishermen usually bring along spinning rods and pails of sardines and snapping shrimp, "just in case" the conditions get difficult.

Al will fish any way you want. He is, after all, a member of the professional redfish tour, and when money is on the line, he says, you're crazy not to use conventional tackle. But back home, on most guide days, he revels in the role of being the captain with the sleek, 18-foot skiff, poling the shallowest water, and setting up for long, accurate fly casts at snook, redfish, and jacks prowling near the mangroves.

"I'll admit, I become a different person when the fish start moving on flies," says Al. "I get excited and pretty worked up. You watch one snook eat a fly like he's supposed to, and then tell me you don't feel the same way."

Al ties on a "Pete's Persuader," checks the leader to make sure it isn't frayed, and hops onto the poling platform to push us toward the east edge of Buttonwood Bay. As promised, we have a perfect falling tide to work with, which means the snook are losing their mangrove cover, inch by inch, making them edgy, but also willing to attack bait retreating along the root edges.

Al runs us through the fishing drill: Cast tight under the branch space near the shoreline, the closer in the better; once the fly hits the water, quickly point the rod tip in the water and start stripping line; work the fly over the drop-offs because there might be rogues cruising the edge; no takers, go again.

We cast the fly into a "U-shaped" shadow along the point. Three quick strips, and a dark brown shape emerges from the mangroves, tracking the streamer like a rocket locked on target. But the fly hesitates slightly (sinking unnaturally), and the snook veers off and returns to his mangrove lair.

"Don't stop the fly!" whispers Al. "If you had something like that chasing you, would you stop? You'd go faster!"

"Sorry, the line slipped."

"That's okay. Try again."

So we do, and the next cast brings a different, larger fish buzzing out from the mangroves, even more aggravated than the first. Five strips, maybe six, and the fish, who can't take it anymore, makes a wide lunge at the fly; as soon as he feels he's been tricked, he thrashes and jumps in frenzied, bass-like arcs around the bow.

"That's what I'm talking about!" smiles Al. "You guys could get used to this snook fishing, eh? I never get tired of watching that happen. Would anybody?"

Snook are snipers and ambush artists. Stealthy, sneaky, nervous, yet still aggressive, they are among the most enigmatic and intriguing of all the sport fish on the flats. A snook's trademark tenacity and acrobatic power are accentuated by its unique physical features: A long, sloping forehead undershot with a shovel-shaped jaw, a wide, fan-like tail and copper pectoral fins, a strangely divided dorsal, and a signature black lateral line that ribbons down both silvery flanks like an interstate median line.

They thrive in warm coastal and brackish waters, and are extremely temperature-sensitive. If the water drops below 60 degrees, they will track to warmer water if possible, even attempt to bury themselves in mud (for warmth) as a final exit strategy, but ultimately, may die. They are homebodies, who never range or migrate too far from a certain area, and like salmon, instinctively return to spawn in the same channels where they were born.

At birth, their only weak defense is transparency. Interestingly, snook are hermaphrodites, born as males, and at certain sizes and ages, some transform into females. The scientific community proposes that the gender transformation occurs in direct proportion to male-to-female ratios within certain groups of fish, somehow creating a healthy, inter-species balance without the direct aid of gender-based competition (Darwinism). Incredibly, if a group of snook is short a few females, they make more.

Females, therefore, are the largest snook. They can live up to 20 years or more, and weigh more than 30 pounds. The non-transforming males can live as long as 15 years, but for any snook to reach significant size is an extreme long shot. A four-year-old fish, maybe two feet long, literally has overcome million-to-one odds in surviving the shallow water threats of dolphins, sharks, and alligators.

Of course, the snook's greatest threat is mankind. Snook populations have experienced significant declines in the last half of the twentieth century as a result of many human pressures in the forms of over-fishing, water diversions and development, and agricultural and industrial pollution. Tougher slot limits and catch quotas implemented in recent years are helping the snook to maintain a fragile balance, but still, their future is decidedly uncertain.

"I've seen snook cruising the beaches of Marco Island, under WaveRunners, even through the legs of people swimming. It shows they're tough, and that they know how to survive," says Al, "but you'd rather see them hunt the mangroves, where they're born into, where they're *meant* to survive."

We ask Al if he had one day to chase any fish in the ocean, what would it be? Without hesitation, he replies, "snook." Although there are schools of tarpon filing through the 10,000 Islands most of the year, permit (considered, by some, the holy grail

of saltwater fly-fishing) and bonefish three or four hours south in the Keys, and acres of bull reds to be caught on the pro redfish tour, Al says he prefers the intimate, one-on-one challenges of the snook.

"I like snook fishing best, because it's like hunting. I live for sight fishing, and in my mind, there's nothing like seeing a big, wild fish out in the open, ready to kill something," he says, smiling down from the platform, still scanning the near waterline with his polarized sunglasses. "You know he's nervous to be up there on the flat in the first place, but the fact that he's willing to risk that exposure means he's on the hunt. You know you have a chance if you can cast well."

He believes that sight fishing for snook has raised the level of his professional ability. He notes that over the years, his approach has become quieter and more streamlined in an effort to consistently slip the boat up on his quarry, all the while, gauging the mood and readiness of the angler on the bow. Every angler is different, some throwing quiet and deadly accurate casts, while others tear up the water and spook fish with sloppy, awkward efforts, he explains.

In any regard, Al says it is *his* responsibility to make everything right before the moment of truth. The confidence of the angler, the position of the boat, the eye line of the guide, the angle of the rod, and the correct fly—all are part of a well-orchestrated act in which Al has control.

"You only get one shot to land the fly on a diagonal line, just inches from a snook's snout. If we do it right, we get rewarded almost every time, but if we're off at all, we'll fail just as easily. The snook is a pretty fair and honest creature, and he's likely to show us, better than I ever can, how our day is fishing."

We have been lucky with the weather, but that is about to end. The wind is pushing against the falling tide, slowing its progress long enough for Al to pole into the shallowest reaches of the bay, and allowing us to squeeze out a few last casts against the mangroves.

Rain drops from a giant storm cell to our south blow across the boat, first as a light, almost refreshing mist, and soon after, with more pelting, stinging intensity. It divides our attention; one moment is spent scanning the bank, looking for fish, the other looking up at the ominous black clouds swirling in our direction.

We hear thunder, and Al is looking for lightning, a bit more intently than the rest of us, probably because he is holding onto a 20-foot graphite stick, which may be one of the best electrical conduits imaginable. He says he's seen lightning hit the water before, and it makes a disturbance like a depth charge.

A few more casts, but no fish, then Al makes the call to get the hell out of here. We are almost too late. As the storm drifts to the east, the winds pinwheel and reverse, accelerating what was left of the falling tide. Within minutes, the water flushes from the bay, dropping the boat into a thin film of oozing mud. Al strains all his weight against the push pole, moving the skiff, foot by foot, off the drying flat.

His cell phone rings. It is an old fisherman, back at the Goodland Marina.

"Son, you'd better get your ass out of there. Have you had a look around?" he says.

"Oh, we see it, and we're on our way!" Al shouts, almost laughing. "Guys, it's time to outrun this storm."

Al poles us off the flat in record time, then quickly fires up the engine, kicking a rooster tail of mud and water behind the boat. The temperature has dropped 20 degrees. The scream of the engine drowns out all noises except the thunderclaps, as we button-hook around a large island, first at the storm, and then straight for home. Nobody has much to say until we come tearing full speed back under the Goodland Bridge and slow at the mouth of the marina.

"I don't think we need a picture of lightning hitting my boat with us in it," Al sighs, visibly relieved, and now smiling. "Maybe we should take a break."

After waiting out the afternoon storms and grabbing some sandwiches back at Marco Island, we decide to fish a few more evening hours, until it gets dark. The tide is now incoming, running against the lower branches of the mangroves, giving the snook an added umbrella of protection from our casts. There is a splash and swirl in the middle of the bay, then another, and another.

"Mullet," Al says. "They'll only play with your mind."

We turn out attention back to the twisted shoreline, making a few blind casts along the way, but the fish are buried well

Al Keller

back in the cover. *Plop.* There's a tiny splash against a root ball. We are about to ask what it is when we look over our shoulders to see Al, standing on the poling platform, digging into his left pocket for another penny. Obviously, he is messing with us, like your kid brother who used to throw rocks in the river when you were learning to fish.

"No, really, check it out," says Al, almost apologetically. "Right now, these snook are buried back in the mangroves, but if they hear something splashing, like injured bait, they'll slide out to have a look. Once they're out in the open, you can throw a fly at them. Here, watch…"

Al finds a small opening in the shoreline, where a deep, sandy channel veins straight against a tangle of fallen vegetation, and throws another penny. We wait, and sure enough, a long, dark shadow begins to patrol the edge of the manufactured disturbance.

Al indicates the success of his experiment with a deep smile, then adds, "Now, don't assume I bribe all my snook with loose change, because I have no intention of being the only Florida flats guide to go broke throwing money at fish."

Al Keller

Al tells us about the time he went trout fishing at the Orvis Guide School in New England, and landed his first trout—a 20-plus-inch brown on a Mickey Finn—then quit river fishing for good, figuring he had little room for improvement. We ask him if he had two weeks, and all the money in the world, where would he go fishing?

"Florida."

He says he'll stay rooted in his home state, and keep exploring the seemingly endless flats and back bays of the northern Everglades, as well as taking time off each summer to tour Florida Bay and the Keys. Spending his whole life here only has made him realize how much there is left to experience.

"You can give me $2,000 and send me to Belize, but what am I going to find there that I can't find here? Permit? We have all the permit anyone will ever need down in the Keys, and bonefish, tarpon, and redfish too."

We tell him about the spectacular redfish in Louisiana, but he already knows.

"Yeah, they have big reds in Louisiana, but it's like every Cajun in the state has each fish memorized and named like extended family. What's the fun in that?

"When it comes to fishing, you have to decide if you like challenges, and I know that I do. I'll take that tougher fish moving across my home water over an easier, exotic fish any day. The harder these fish get to catch, the harder I'll work to figure them out. I don't ever see myself leaving south Florida because I got outworked by a snook or tarpon."

A manatee pokes its nose and eyes above the surface, maybe 20 yards away, just to check us out, then slinks off towards the Gulf in a graceful, heavy shadow. Two bull sharks trail the manatee, either hunting or observing the large, plant-eating mammal. The size of the sharks officially rules out any ill-conceived swimming plans for later this evening, regardless of whether the resort says the ocean is "safe" or not.

It is common to see sharks on the flats adjacent to the Gulf, drawn by the abundance of prey and the incoming tide cycles. Al says enough bull, lemon, nurse, blacktip, and hammerhead sharks frequent these shallows that nobody ever should consider "wetting a toe" no matter how hot the weather gets.

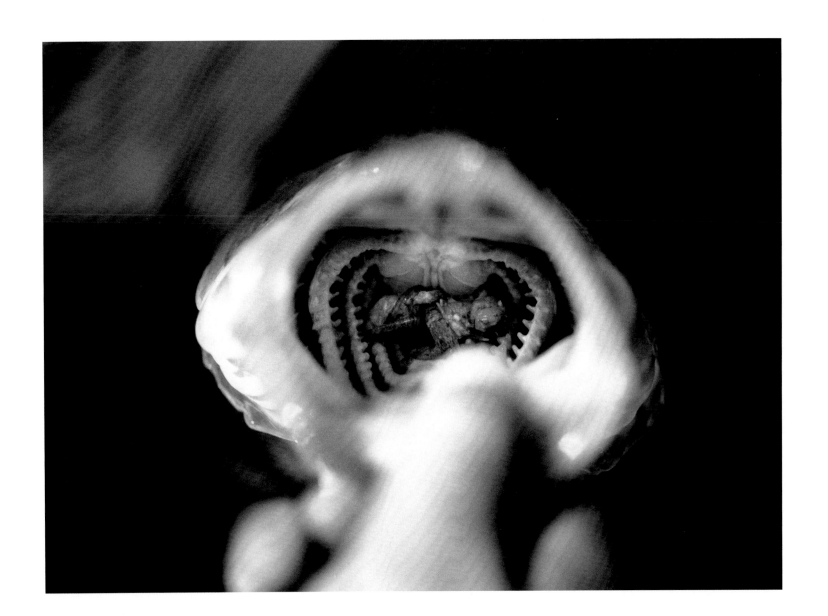

"If these Marco Island tourists took a good look down at all the sharks swimming below their feet while parasailing, they'd never get in the water again. I tell *all* my clients that there's nothing wrong with using the pool to cool off."

Later, Al stares over the side of the skiff and notices a small nurse shark cruising under the engine. He drops off the platform, plunges his hand into the discolored water, and snatches the small shark off the bottom with one hand. He holds up the stunned, brown fish with a smile, then drops it back in the water unharmed.

"You need to teach a shark at young age that he's got something to fear, otherwise he'll just grow up to be a big bully."

We spend the final morning with another falling tide, getting in a few last casts on the bays among the red mangrove islands. In another hour or two, it will be back to the dock, back to civilization, the airport, and finally, home. This has been a long trip.

We have shots at a few, large redfish, and catch a mangrove snapper. A 40-pound tarpon rolls not far down the flat, and we give him a few half-hearted shots, then refocus on the shoreline.

"I'm looking forward to a few days off," says Al. "It's been so stormy lately, but it seems like when the tide is right, the weather is wrong, and when the skies are clear, the tide's back up."

"You poor fellow, how do you cope?" It is refreshing when you know a guide well enough that you can begin to give him a little payback harassment.

"Oh, I think I'll manage."

Maybe it is the light atmosphere, or that the guiding pressure is off, but a big snook slams the fly, then tears about the surface near the boat. Al thinks we should end the trip on this fish.

On the run back to the Goodland Marina, we notice that the sandy mouths of the snook have worn against our thumbprints. Scratchy thumbprints, memories of running wide open beneath summer storms, throwing pennies at snook, and sharing time with a good friend will be the only trophies we will take home from the 10,000 Islands.

That is plenty.

Outrun A Storm

For an hour an east wind has held the outgoing tide
on a two hundred acre mangrove flat, enough water to keep
decent schools of mullet from tearing off for their lives,
and amber-stone-finned snook ready to kill crippled silversides.
When the wind shifts then dies, like it does before
an afternoon storm, the remnants of tide and loitering snook
fall away and vanish for good. Eight inches of water left
on the mangrove flat, if you're lucky, so you better get poling
your ass off, because this storm to the east is dark grey,
full of lightning, and looks like a wet, cracked blackboard.
Five minutes to make it to a prop scar, start the lower unit,
and get running flat out home. Run a white-capped inlet
into the cool wall of mainland air. Run two no-wake zones
under the storm edge because the manatees can get the hell
out of the way. Run the deserted causeway because you
don't want to see what this lightning would do to us or the skiff.
By the time the storm sweeps in like grass fire, we take cover
under one of the marina's decrepit verandas. Through a torn
screen door in the corner, an old fisherman drinking beer
with a badly eroded face says he seen us outrun the storm
and reckons it's luck or grace of God that we made it back alive.
We say, it's the Captain's job to get us in alive. He says,
don't be foolish, everyone knows that's the job of the good Lord.

Conway Bowman
San Diego, California

The last stop on the "Sanity Express" may well be "the 182," a nondescript point on a GPS map twenty-some miles off the coast of San Diego. It is here, heaving through the swells in an 18-foot Parker skiff, with a burlap chum bag hanging off the side, waiting for mako sharks to arrive, where we start to think that, maybe, this whole fly-fishing adventure has gone a bit too far.

There is something profoundly disturbing about crossing the line from chasing "gamefish" to chasing apex predators that not only are capable of killing you, but also may have a strong interest in killing you. In many ways, fly-fishing for sharks on the open Pacific is something of a professional and personal reckoning, one that will leave you questioning your physical limits and those of your tackle, your personal safety, and, finally, your own sanity. Although

unlikely, there always is the possibility that you might not make it back from your first shark fishing trip.

Unfazed by these risks, Conway Bowman decided nearly ten years ago to specialize in catching sharks on fly rods, shortfin makos to be exact. The absurdity of this little hobby has earned him considerable coast-to-coast acclaim. While we half expected Conway to be the ultimate X-Games outcast with an adrenaline habit, within the first five minutes on his boat we found someone altogether different. Meticulously preparing his boat and tackle for the day's fishing, Conway is a technician and surgeon. He also carries himself with a balance, confidence, and California coolness that never smacks of feigned bravery or bravado. His eyes are sharp and blue, and often look straight through you.

For Conway, his life among the sharks has legitimate cause. On the coast of southern California, there aren't hordes of trout, tarpon, or bonefish, but there are plenty of makos. As a young outdoorsman from San Diego with a genuine passion for fly-fishing, Conway realized early on that, for better or worse, you fish for what's in your backyard.

"We all have our own fish. Makos are my ultimate fish," he says. "It means something when you tie into a fish that can fight back with something more than just a pull on your line. A mako can kill you, and that changes the whole game."

Most good fisherman, when they can't be on the water, go someplace where they can *think* about fishing. Conway makes a point to take us to Stroud's tackle, where he introduces us to his "surrogate parents," Bill and Eileen Stroud, who have run a small fly shop in the heart of urban San Diego for the past 35 years. Conway recalls many afternoons ratting around this shop, kicking over boxes, looking at pictures, as his father, John Bowman, and Bill Stroud shared stories from Alaska, Montana, and Northern California's spring creeks.

John Bowman taught his son how to trout fish during summers their family spent at Redfish Lodge in central Idaho. To this day, Mr. Bowman is proud to have placed an early "diversion" in Conway's life (originally meant to keep him out of trouble) that since has grown into a source of sport, income, and natural wonder.

The visit to Stroud's is like a trip with the middleweight champ back to the neighborhood gym where it all started. Conway still treasures this place and these people with uncommon reverence, and he credits his father and the Strouds for fueling his passion. Bill Stroud claims he tried to warn Conway away from fishing as a way of life, often remarking, "Don't do it, it'll ruin you!" but soon learned that Conway was an independent young man who would make his own decisions. Conway says he respected the advice of his uncle Bill, but knew fishing was something he had to do.

So Conway bought an old 17-foot aluminum skiff, read everything outdoor writer Nick Curcione had to say about mako fishing, and began spending his days pressing further and further offshore in search of sharks. With only a compass for navigation,

it took Conway two years to land his first mako. In hindsight, he admits these self-taught shark lessons were dangerous, but very effective.

Conway now stands as the California icon of shark fishing with the fly. He has been written up in numerous magazines and newspapers, has been on television shows, and has clients from all over the country. There is no counting the number of world record size fish that have been caught on Conway's boat—fish that never will be listed in an IGFA record book because he doesn't concern himself with tapes and scales, and is adamant about letting every fish go. Yet Conway is humble about his many accomplishments.

"For me, being famous for fishing, or being known as the best fishing guide, is about as noteworthy as being the tallest midget in the world."

Fly-fishing for sharks is a fairly straight-forward operation. It starts by finding a spot, like the 182, where the ocean floor drops or shelves off abruptly, which creates habitat for the schools of mackerel, skip-jacks, albacore, and the pelagics that chase

them. Once there, you check the current, plan a drift of several miles over the shelf, set a blood and chum slick, then wait.

Everything on the shark drift feels small—the boat, your gear, the birds, even the clouds overhead. It is an unsettling smallness, exaggerated by the contrast of gray ocean expanse and the enormous creatures that swim here. The concussive blowing of blue whales sounds near the horizon, and we only can sit and watch, awestruck, as they roll into view, like black 737s melting over the ocean's surface and exhaling clouds of spray.

Conway watches cautiously. If the whales get beneath us inadvertently, they could toss our boat over like a cork, without ever realizing or caring that we are here. The whales pass without fanfare, and Conway begins slicing up an albacore carcass with a rusted knife and stuffs it into a burlap sack. The sacks are placed in plastic milk crates, then hung over the side of the boat.

"That's it boys. No swimming from now on," smiles Captain Dave Trimble from the chase boat.

Captain Dave is 23, energetic, handsome, and still at the stage of life where everything is about the pursuit. Whether cruising for California women in his classic rag-top Cadillac, running all night on offshore albacore trips, fashioning mannequin-on-surfboard teasers for white sharks, or helping Conway fill in his summer mako charters, life is "all good" for Captain Dave. Captain Dave has spent the last year helping Conway run shark charters, earning a reputation as a young, dedicated, brash, and hard working new captain. Conway likes his style, but most importantly, respects his work ethic.

"Captain Dave's dream is to pull on a 'Whitey' with a fly rod…I just want to make sure I'm out of the state when it happens."

In truth, the great white doesn't have much on the mako, other than size and reputation.

They both are killing machines. The mako might be more efficient than the great white. He is faster, and can swim up to 60 miles per hour, placing him in the top handful of fish, along with the swordfish and the wahoo, for speed. There are other unique features that differentiate the mako as a premier hunter and predator.

Conway describes their "Messerschmitt" bodies as muscular, compact, powerful, and superbly efficient. Their eyes point forward. Unlike other sharks, they do not have protective skin flaps or eyelids, meaning they have to bite to kill, and avoid violent struggles with their prey. The loss of an eye is a death sentence for a mako in the open ocean. The fuselage is lean but thick, and it tapers down in abrupt curves to the tail, joining power and control in one precise point. Their fins are understated, offering a stealthy ride through water.

A mako shark's mouth is a mangled array of teeth that point and overlap in conflicting patterns, like bent and twisted strands of razor wire. They seem disorganized and random, but this actually is a virtue of evolution. Unlike other sharks that might stun, or bite, or scavenge in three or four steps, the mako hunts and kills in one fluid motion. His teeth allow him to deliver the death blow, hold on, and consume in one pass.

The mako has a killer instinct that starts before birth, as the unborn pups literally kill and feed off of weaker siblings *in utero*. This gives the ones that are born an edge to surviving the infinite threats that abound in bluewater.

But what sets the mako apart from all other fish is his brain. Roughly the size of a cat's brain (uncommonly large by fish standards), the mako's brain seems to give him the most necessary hunter's attribute—cunning. In fact, Conway says all makos behave somewhat differently than others, making them respectably unpredictable, as if they have their own personalities.

We notice a stillness near the boat. The birds have flown away. Conway cups the brim of his hat and stares into the chum slick.

"He's here," Conway utters. "I know it. It might take him 45 minutes to work his way into view, but he's here, checking us out. I can feel it."

There are different ways you can find a mako shark, or have him find you. You can look for blue water, find dislodged kelp and bait, and watch for terns. Conway says terns gliding and diving near the boat are good telltales that sharks are in the area. While gulls are scavengers, chasing baitfish and picking at junk and debris, terns are more deliberate. They like to eat fresh afterkill the makos leave behind as they feed through schools of fish.

Sometimes, you chance upon "finners," makos cruising along the surface in lazy hunt mode. But they aren't easy to spot with their compact, rounded dorsal fins, and they seldom telegraph their presence.

With a chum slick spread out in an oily film behind the boat, Conway sporadically casts a mackerel carcass with a spinning rod in random directions around the boat, and retrieves the teaser with a fast skitter along the surface. For the most part, this is casting practice. Every now and again, the dragging dead bait brings a swirl, a slash, or a sleek, black shadow tracking toward the boat, but more often, the mako shows up on his own terms.

You can be chatting, eating a sandwich, or just killing time when the scene abruptly changes. You quickly notice the small blue sharks pecking at the chum bag have disappeared. There is an eerie calm.

A slate profile with black marble eyes makes a glide-by run a scant few arm lengths from the boat, close enough to look right in your eyes and make the hair on the back of your neck stand up. It isn't fear, and it isn't adrenaline. It is awe.

Unlike most fish that get a good look at

the boat and spook, the mako doesn't swim faster or get nervous in the presence of humans. He just stays, checking you out, calculating his next move. Conway says a mako will hover within a stone's throw of the boat for a good half hour, maybe longer, just taking his time, waiting for something to happen.

"Makos know they are at the top of the food chain out here. When they come in close to the boat, they wonder where *we* fit in."

There is no maelstrom of human energy when the mako shows, unlike what you might expect. In other offshore situations, like billfish charters, the arrival of a fish means the boat goes electric—bluewater mates jump to life, the deck sings with action, rods crank up, voices yell, and engines begin downshifting. But Conway Bowman always measures his mako, and this is a fish that measures you back. Everything drops to a calm, deliberate hush. Words become scarce; there is only the sound of swells lapping against the hull, and all eyes are trained overboard.

"There he is… what an awesome fish,"

Conway whispers. "This one is a slug, a real gorilla. 160 pounds, maybe better."

Conway is calculating. Slowly, quietly, he grabs the teaser rod, and makes ready for a cast. We'll have to work this fish up, make him mad, if we are going to get him to eat a fly. After the shark makes two or three passes by the boat, Conway confirms his choice of fly rod. We'll use the 15-weight, the big one.

Most "catchable" makos are adolescents, ranging between 50 and 150 pounds. The waters off San Diego are one of the few prime breeding grounds on the globe where these fish are found in abundance. The chum slick, however, does not discriminate between "big" and "little," and it is not unusual to bring in a large female mako (over 400 hundred pounds), or even a great white. This spring, Captain Dave had an eighteen foot great white eat a 90-pound Pacific white-sided dolphin twenty feet behind the transom.

We ask Conway what equipment he would consider using to deal with a 400-pound mako.

"When they get that big, I grab the camera and leave the rods alone."

After you have fished enough offshore situations, you come to anticipate the instantaneous runs, the thunderous charges, and the straight-to-the-air acrobatics of pelagic fish. A mako often will not do that.

A mako is used to eating things that try to fight back, stick him, hurt him, and scar the insides of his mouth. Your brightly-colored shark fly is the equivalent of small, harmless baitfish, a lunch snack, or an "M&M." So there is lag time, even after you watch the mako eat the fly and start swimming away with colorful red tassles draped out of the corner of his mouth.

This lag time lasts about 30 seconds, although in your head, it seems to last an hour. All you do at this point is hold the fly line taught in your hand. It is a fine balance. Not enough tension, and the mako will spit out the fly. Too much and he will break you clean off with the first slash of his tail. When you hold it right, you are letting him stick himself, digging the fly deep into a scarce soft pit in the corner of his mouth.

Sometimes, despite your best effort, the fly wraps around a mangled tooth, of which the mako has many. All it takes is a head shake and the fly pops loose. The consola-tion in this case is that the hard-mouthed fish doesn't feel anything, and if he did, he doesn't care. More than likely, he will come back for another grab.

Properly hooked and held tight (enough for him to finally feel some resistance), the mako senses something is wrong, and this is one of the very few times in his life when he goes on the defense, becoming a vicious, unpredictable fighter.

He will run and charge, and if you're lucky, cartwheel and throw himself across the ocean with violent indiscretion. You must be careful to keep him and his gnashing teeth from jumping in the boat. Sometimes, he'll jump and flop over on the line, cutting himself free with a clean slice of his tail. Usually, he fights almost to the death, holding his ground, insulted and aggravated.

"The only time the shark loses his trade-mark discipline is when he's in the air. It is an awesome encounter, because that's the one moment when he is out of his world."

Conway grabs the leader and pulls the fish alongside the boat. He lifts its sub-stantial head, tilting up its black snout, and dropping the jaws to reveal a paint-can-sized mouth of ugly teeth. With his other hand, he slides a self-designed hook release tool along the steel leader, over the fly, and with a pop, the hook comes loose and the big, blue-gray fish cruises angrily away. This dirty ballet is over, and nobody got hurt.

As the day wears on, the sharks come and go in spurts. An hour of nothing… three fins pouring down a swell at the boat… a missed hookset… another missed hookset… *another* missed hookset. More nothing… Finally, a fish caught. We never feel comfortable, but we start to lose our fear, wrapped up in the fascination of these mako sharks and their acrobatic grace.

Likewise, we grow comfortable with Conway. His genuine nature and his passion cannot help but instill a sense of admiration, not born of skill, but of his respect for the environment he works. These clearly are his fish. His friends. He says he sees himself in the makos.

"These are elusive fish, a lot like me. Sometimes they like me, sometimes they don't. I truly believe that the makos are sensitive to someone's energy. Good energy on the boat means a good day with the sharks.

I know when a guy on the boat has bad vibes. Not to get too weird, or California 'new age' on you or anything, but it's important to understand.

"It's a very primal thing when you come into this world with the makos."

Things of this world evolve: sharks, rivers, oceans, even anglers.

So it seems that Conway Bowman also will evolve down another path, sooner rather than later, he says. It isn't that he's done with makos, or learning about them. It is the opposite; he says he wants to spend less time fishing and more time observing, like the very first days, when he would sit on his aluminum boat and watch these magnificent creatures circle around, without ever lifting a rod to cast.

"I want to be an amateur scientist," he says. "Spend more time studying and tagging these makos, rather than trying to aggravate them."

He plans to give Captain Dave the keys to the kingdom. The clients, the referrals, the business—even the secret list of anglers who get the "local" treatment, a.k.a. a day spent in unproductive water

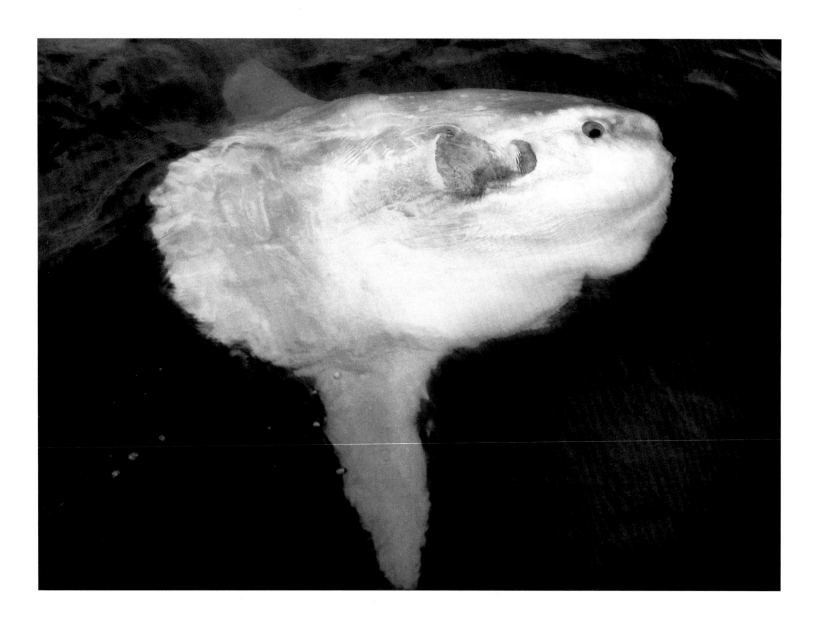

filled with just enough blue sharks to keep anglers excited, without really showing them prized mako locations.

And he will look for new adventures in new water. Maybe roosterfish in Baja or the Rio Santo Domingo trout in Mexico. But San Diego always will call him back, in one way or another, if only to run down a finner, or spend an afternoon in Stroud's shop.

Conway is proud of the fact that the commercial fishermen and day charter captains never quite figured out what or why he does what he does. "Hey, *River Runs Through It*... How'd it go?" the commercial skippers whistle and laugh when Conway putters his little skiff back into the Dana Landing.

It all is fine. Everyone finds their own niche. The ocean is big enough for all of us, Conway says.

"I have the same recurring dream, about sharks, every now and again.

"In this dream I am fighting the sharks. They are swimming all around me, in big circles. Everywhere I look, I see sharks.

"I am battling them as hard as I can, and always... always, the sharks win.

"But I am not afraid. I am never afraid.

"It isn't a violent, bloody battle, but they get me, one piece at a time, and still, I am not afraid.

"And I just go down fighting. And after the last punch is thrown, it's like I just concede, okay, you won... it's cool.

"I have tried to understand and interpret this dream, and the best I can imagine is that it shows the difference between fear and respect. Respect is different than fear, but no less powerful.

"Fishermen go after a certain quarry. It becomes their job. And my quarry has become the shark.

"Over the years, you begin to live vicariously through your quarry, and I have begun to live vicariously through these sharks.

"I think that's ultimately why they cooperate with me.

"I respect them, and they respect me."

Mako

A shark can smell a drop of blood in twenty thousand
gallons of water, but no one has the slightest idea
when a mako will show, anyone who does should be picking horses.
We are prepared to wait seven minutes or seven hours
for a fifty to a hundred and fifty pound adolescent.
Everyone is praying we avoid a large female or great white.
Once, a seven-foot female came finning straight back
at the captain's boat, disappeared under the engine
(shearing off an eighteen-weight fly line on the trim plate),
then cartwheeled five times into an overcast horizon.
"Whitey" ate a ninety-pound dolphin behind the transom
this spring, and these baby bonito sharks
can be real pit bulls when they put their mouths
on the prop to taste electricity coming off the zinc anode.
Captain says, if a mako gets in the boat,
everyone grab a gaff, and we get her ass back in the water,
OK? because no one's swimming back from here.
A mako's uncovered eyes are pitch-black desert obsidian;
their teeth are clear plastic flames; their backs, blue and grey sandpaper.
When they wish, makos straight-line or launch
themselves at offshore clouds with car accident velocity.
Does anyone know why we fish for these creatures?

All The Captain's Boys

All the Captain's boys are asleep in the dunes and grass
beside the jetty, where they dream of the sea.
The mountains they dream are not mountains,
but the flukes and spines of whales ordered against the horizon.
The shelling of war they dream is not the shelling of war,
but the unmerciful, iron surf pounding the shoreline.
The screeching of children they dream is not the screeching of children,
but the calls of herring gulls grating over the breakers.
The thousands of stars they dream are not thousands of stars,
but countless phosphorescent jellyfish floating out on a midnight tide.
All the Captain's boys dream of being Captains
like their father, and their father's father, and their father's father's father.
To wake them is to take their warm, unmarked hands,
to gaze into the burning blue brine of their eyes,
to hold their prayers bound with poverty-grass one final time.
They have waited all their lives to not return
from the freak seas and fishing accidents that will ruin them.
When they head into the giant nor'easter off Amagansett,
rubbing down their arms and hands with ashes,
hoping to fill their nets with writhing piles of bass and weakfish,
all the Captain's boys say they smell fish in the wind.
But the wind they smell has black, serpent-like eyes,
and races across the night sky like a comet.
The wind they smell is an Amagansett wind,
and an Amagansett wind cannot save them.

Plates

(listed by page number)